# Learning To Walk

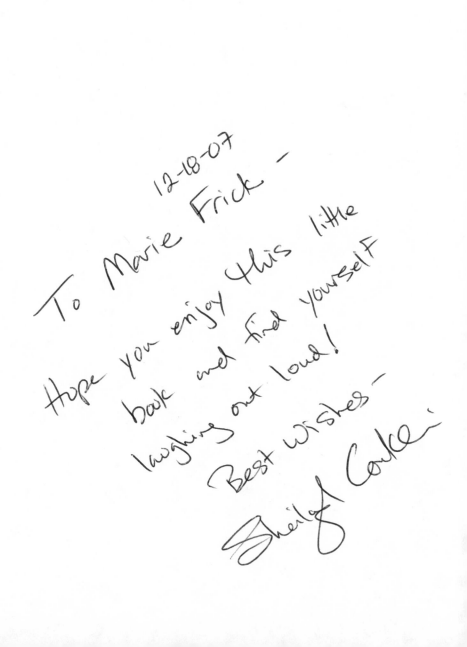

12-18-07

To Marie Frick —

Hope you enjoy this little book and find yourself laughing out loud!

Best wishes —

Sheila Conklin

# Learning To Walk

✦

## From the Sofa to a Marathon in Nine Months

*Sheilagh Conklin*

iUniverse, Inc.

New York  Lincoln  Shanghai

# Learning To Walk
## From the Sofa to a Marathon in Nine Months

iUniverse books may be ordered through booksellers or by contacting:

iUniverse
2021 Pine Lake Road, Suite 100
Lincoln, NE 68512
www.iuniverse.com
1-800-Authors (1-800-288-4677)

Because of the dynamic nature of the Internet, any Web addresses or links contained in this book may have changed since publication and may no longer be valid.

ISBN: 978-0-595-45436-5 (pbk)
ISBN: 978-0-595-89749-0 (ebk)

Printed in the United States of America

For Jon.

# Contents

Preface . . . . . . . . . . . . . . . . . . . . . . . . . . . . . . . . . . . . . . . . . . . . . . . . . xi

I Am Fat: The Supporting Evidence . . . . . . . . . . . . . . . . . . . . . . . . . 1

What Do I Know? Next to Nothing . . . . . . . . . . . . . . . . . . . . . . . . . 5

Packing the Fanny Pack . . . . . . . . . . . . . . . . . . . . . . . . . . . . . . . . . 7

First Day of Training: Lapped By the Elderly and Other Humiliating
    Lessons . . . . . . . . . . . . . . . . . . . . . . . . . . . . . . . . . . . . . . . . . . . 9

Stretching and Sweating: Athlete or Pig? . . . . . . . . . . . . . . . . . . . . 11

Personal Space: Thongs and Locker Rooms . . . . . . . . . . . . . . . . . . 13

Do You Flock? . . . . . . . . . . . . . . . . . . . . . . . . . . . . . . . . . . . . . . . 16

March Progress Report: Getting Off My Ass . . . . . . . . . . . . . . . . . . 18

Trophy Wife . . . . . . . . . . . . . . . . . . . . . . . . . . . . . . . . . . . . . . . . . 21

The Misunderstood Undergarment of the Very Thin . . . . . . . . . . . . 23

Athlete Without a Team . . . . . . . . . . . . . . . . . . . . . . . . . . . . . . . . . 26

Second in Command of Two . . . . . . . . . . . . . . . . . . . . . . . . . . . . . 29

April Progress Report: Sheilagh's Dreidel Diet . . . . . . . . . . . . . . . . 31

Weight Loss and Rocket Science . . . . . . . . . . . . . . . . . . . . . . . . . . . 34

An Exercise-Induced Imaginary Adventure . . . . . . . . . . . . . . . . . . . 37

My Invisible Friend, Farrokh, Queen of Mile Two . . . . . . . . . . . . . . 40

Watch Your Step: Parenting a Pre-teen Daughter . . . . . . . . . . . . . . . 43

May Progress Report: Calories, Healthy Habits, and Becoming
    Neurotic . . . . . . . . . . . . . . . . . . . . . . . . . . . . . . . . . . . . . . . . . 46

Hydration, Toenails and Other Warnings . . . . . . . . . . . . . . . . . . . 49

Poisoning a Previously Perpetually Polluted Person . . . . . . . . . . . . . 54

Summer Progress Report: Injured, Shoeless, but Still Walking. . . . . . . 56

Personal Parts and Pieces . . . . . . . . . . . . . . . . . . . . . . . . . . . . . . . 59

On Your Mark . . . . . . . . . . . . . . . . . . . . . . . . . . . . . . . . . . . . . . . 62

Get Set . . . . . . . . . . . . . . . . . . . . . . . . . . . . . . . . . . . . . . . . . . . . 65

Go! . . . . . . . . . . . . . . . . . . . . . . . . . . . . . . . . . . . . . . . . . . . . . . 69

That's A Wrap! . . . . . . . . . . . . . . . . . . . . . . . . . . . . . . . . . . . . . . 76

My Marathon Nightmare . . . . . . . . . . . . . . . . . . . . . . . . . . . . . . . 81

# *Acknowledgments*

This improbable journey was not my idea. I must, therefore, begin by acknowledging and thanking the remarkable, dedicated, pushy woman who dragged me off the couch and pushed me toward Portland, Karen Corrigan—my niece, business partner, editor, and friend. Thank you.

The Children's Tumor Foundation Marathon Team puts meaning into every step as they race to find the cure for neurofibromatosis. Their passion is infectious. Since this organization and the kids they are helping were my catalysts for change, I am donating five percent of the proceeds I receive from the sale of this book to the Children's Tumor Foundation.

I am so fortunate to have many good friends who either cheered me on or walked beside me each step of the way, mile after painful mile. I appreciate your energy, your willingness to laugh at my jokes, your donations to the Children's Tumor Foundation, and your steady friendship. Special thanks go to Patty Allen and her daughter, Elizabeth; Rena Peterson and her daughter, Rianne; Susan Cooper and her daughter, Claire; Jeanette Rust and her daughters, Shannon and Alison; Lisa Kostal and her daughter, Talia; Lynda and John Turner; and Lisa Neshyba and her daughter, Veronica. And thanks to Vicki Bergevin and Corinne McNeely for encouraging me to continue this project and the years of unwavering friendship.

My family is simply amazing. Our kids are incredible. Morgan, Mara, Laurie, and Henry walked many miles by my side while Riley, Jack and Kevin offered support and hugs at the end of long days. My siblings and their spouses also helped by laughing at the right times, encouraging me to keep writing, and giving generous donations. Much love goes to Gina Laughney, Brian Kelberg, John Laughney, Diane Mayfield, Lauren Madrid, and most especially Sean Laughney, one of the nicest and funniest people I know. And of course, there's my mother, Mary Laughney. I am so grateful for her unconditional love, her gentle editing advice, and the support she sends my way no matter what crazy things I say or do. She is an irreplaceable gift to me, and I'm so thankful that she's my Mom.

Finally, there is Jon. We have one of those amazing, effortless marriages full of trust, respect, love, and kindness. He is my heart, and I love him completely. Thank you, Jon, for everything you are and everything you do.

# Preface

In February of 2006 my business partner, Karen, signed me on to the Children's Tumor Foundation's Marathon Team in anticipation of doing the Portland Marathon in October. Nothing could be more out of character for me. It was an outrageous idea with no basis in reality. In my mid-forties and more than a bit overweight, I was not in shape and not athletic. Not only that, I had no history of athleticism. Even as a kid or young adult I was not into sports, working out, or jogging. The closest I got was buying leggings in the early eighties after watching "Flashdance".

As I began to tell people I was going to do the Portland Marathon, all asked the same question. Why? Good question, but I had no answer. Then one quiet day when all the kids were at school, I sat at my desk, stared at my blank computer screen, and asked myself the same question. "Why?"

I took a deep breath and wrote three words. I am fat.

Initially I just stared at the words. Then my fingers started typing, and my thoughts flowed onto the screen. It wasn't long before I found myself writing and smiling. It felt good to unload onto the computer. But what was really fun to discover was that my internal dialog was kind of funny. At least I thought so. At times I was even laughing out loud, especially in subsequent essays. This process of dumping my thoughts into a Word document had me squarely face the sobering reality of my poor physical state of affairs while tapping into my sense of humor at the same time.

After a few pages I sat back and read what I had written—truthful thoughts and feelings bound together by humor. I liked what I read. This is not only what I think but how I think. Without too much editing or rewriting, I had put forth an accurate explanation, in a voice that sounded authentically my own, of why I was going to do the Portland Marathon. I had never written anything like this before. Best of all, it was rather easy to do. And, it gave me a sense of wellness. And, it was free. What could be better than an easy, free, painless, wellness activity?

I decided to email my first essay to a couple of friends. They immediately wrote back—they loved it! If I write anything more, I should pass it along. I hadn't thought about writing more, but why not? I sat down the next week and wrote out my thoughts again. I emailed them, adding a couple of other friends to the list, and received nothing but encouragement and applause. "Keep writing!" I did.

Soon my journal had an email list of about 30 people, young and old, men and women. All the essays hang together and, over nine months, served to pull me toward the Portland Marathon. When I was done I put them into a single document. I was shocked. I had written 26 essays plus a short little dream at the end. A marathon is 26 miles plus a short little .2 mile piece at the end. How likely is that? This was definitely a sign.

# I Am Fat: The Supporting Evidence

I am fat.

I am dedicating the second half of my life to better health. I say this now with full conviction. Since it's February, January must be over, and it's a good bet this is not merely a tired New Year's resolution that has stuck around too long. This is something different. I have no choice. I've been cornered by my own bad habits. This corner I find myself in has no way out except through a single door, and I can't fit through it unless I act.

I am fat. I can not use big bones, large build, dense muscles, thyroid malfunction, post partum, slow metabolism or any other glandular excuse. I am fat because I ate too much. I must decide to either stay in my fat corner, living life as a fat person, or suck it up and waddle through the door marked "change" and do what it takes to reclaim my inner babe.

My experiences with and choices regarding clothing are sure signs that I'm trying in vain to hide about 50 extra pounds, the size of a typical six-year-old. I have not tucked a shirt into my jeans in over a decade, assuming that wearing a baggy long shirt down to the middle of my backside will somehow make me look svelte. My jeans are huge and my underpants are the size of a small pup tent. Putting on pantyhose is an ugly affair. The contortions are painful to perform and worse to witness. It's so bad that I have sunk to a new low of buying knee highs. I've given up the panty part. I no longer try to gather my midsection and force it into the control top of a pair of queen-size pantyhose. Tying shoes causes blood flow issues. Doubling over at the waist is like compressing my adipose first grader to the point where my eyes feel like they're popping out of my head.

The physical signs of being fat are undeniable and impossible to hide despite efforts to cover, drape, tuck, conceal, control or mask. Throughout my first thirty years I prided myself on having a flat stomach. Now, I must lean far forward to see my toes, and a side view confirms that six months pregnant would be a good guess to describe my silhouette. Thighs rub together mercilessly. When standing, there is no space between my legs at the crotch. You must go to my knees before

1

any rays of daylight can find their way through. Hips have several handles to choose from. I am now plucking hairs off two chins. When seated, I can hoist one leg over the other but only such that the ankle of the top leg is resting on the knee of the other—neither feminine nor comfortable. There are no more discrete, out-of-the-way locations on my body to quietly hide the accumulation of chub. It is layering on every square inch it can gain purchase.

And then there are the raw, hard numbers that describe my physique—height, weight, and all the measurements that quantify the various circumferences of pertinent body parts. My personal stats are, to say the least, impressive. One good thing has evolved because of this, my math skills have sharpened. Knowing that my addition to a full elevator is significant, I do some fast calculations and estimations to insure the equipment is up to the task.

Professional sports have many indicators that my height/weight ratio resides on the far right of the human bell curve. The recent Winter Olympics confirms that I am equivalent to two male ski jumpers. Several players on the Seattle Seahawks starting squad are smaller than me.

My husband loves to watch baseball and has noticed that most major league teams have what he describes as a fat pitcher in the line up. Sometimes he's a relief pitcher, sometimes a closer. They have round faces, chubby jowls, thick arms, and bellies that push against their uniforms and hang over their belt. They don't run from the bull pen to the mound when called up. My husband tries to predict when the team will turn to the fat pitcher during the ebb and flow of a game. During one game last season he proclaimed, "I knew it! They're bringing in their fat pitcher!" The TV announcer comments as well, stating that the player is a big guy, five feet eight inches tall and two hundred eight pounds. I am fatter than the fat pitcher.

To move ahead I must first acknowledge that weight reduction is not an impossibly complicated task. This is not to say it won't be hard, it just shouldn't be complicated. It was certainly simple enough to get here so reversing the equation shouldn't be beyond my capability.

The "Getting Fat Equation" = Eating too much of the wrong stuff + Shunning anything remotely healthy + Decreasing my activity level with each passing year.

The "Getting Thinner Equation" = Dramatically reducing the consumption of the wrong stuff + Consuming healthy foods + Increasing my activity level ASAP.

My list of wrong stuff is easy to put together: chips, chocolate, cookies, candy, croissants, crackers, and cake. In short, I appear to love all things starting with c.

I know what the healthy foods are, I just need to learn to love and appreciate them. I didn't eat my first salad until I was 30. If I don't eat a piece of fruit soon I'll be the first person in a century to contract scurvy. I need to modify my view of fruits and vegetables. My internal dialog has nothing good to say about veggies, salad, fresh fruit and whole grains. In fact, when I hear people exclaim excitement at the site of a salad or fruit plate, I wonder who they're trying to kid. I must learn to squeal with delight when faced with the opportunity to eat raw vegetables. I will fake it at first and hope that successful weight management will turn my opinion around. This will be the single most difficult factor in my successful completion of the "Getting Thinner Equation".

Increasing my activity level is something I'm looking forward to. I hate the term "working out" so I'm not going to use it, ever. I'm going to get moving. To cement my commitment to an increase in activity level, I was recently bamboozled into signing up to do the Portland Marathon, seven months from now. Granted, I get winded walking to my neighbor's, but I have tremendous confidence in my ability to change from sedentary chubster to mobile athlete. To be honest, I plan on "doing" the Portland Marathon, not "running" the Portland Marathon—a big difference. My goal is to walk 26.2 miles in one day without stopping and before the sun sets. The training schedule I found for a novice marathon walker is detailed and manageable. I will use this for my "increase activity" part of the equation.

And finally, for me, goal setting is a critical part of success. I need concrete, measurable goals. No grey area. Either I achieve my goal or I don't. They must be reasonable and attainable, meaningful and pleasurable. My six goals are:

- Tuck in a shirt, put on a belt, and be pleased enough with the resulting look that I go to my local grocery store and do the shopping.

- Get up off the floor without the aid of furniture. Simply stand up.

- Sit on the edge of the bed, roll up a non-queen size pair of pantyhose to the toe, bring my knee straight up, put my foot in, and slide the hose up my leg. No extra movements or contortions.

- Perform a slow jog on the treadmill in front of the large mirrors at the health club and maintain it such that my ponytail bobs and swings back and forth in a cute, perky fashion. Having had short hair for most of my fat period, I'm growing out my hair in anticipation of meeting this goal.

- Put on a tennis dress, pick up my racket, walk onto the tennis court and play doubles with the ladies.

- Wear a cute pair of girly panties that ride on my hips (versus utilitarian cotton whites that come well up onto my waist).

Yes, I have backed myself right into the fat corner. But acknowledging this at 45 gives me hope that I can have a fat chapter in my life, versus a fat life. It's now time to say good-bye to my adipose first grader and put her down because the two of us can't fit through the door of the changing room together. And there's no way I'm carrying her 26.2 miles around Portland in October.

# *What Do I Know? Next to Nothing*

The more I think about it, the more I like it—Sheilagh doing a marathon. A full fledge, Greek Olympian, beg for mercy, no wimps allowed marathon.

This is what I know. I know that a marathon is 26.2 miles, an odd distance that must equate to some even number in the metric system. I know that my training plan leading up to marathon day will increase my exercise level 1000 percent. I know that I should probably invest in some good sneakers. This is all I know about a marathon.

I bet there are books written about marathon strategy and psychology, magazines dedicated to the art of marathon training and pacing, and papers written by nutrition experts explaining the effects of carbo-loading, protein balancing, hydration requirements, and metabolite replenishment. And there are undoubtedly many companies trying to sell you their products to enhance the marathon experience—shoes, socks, shorts, bras, energy bars, energy drinks, energy tablets, energy patches, energy gum, etc.

I, however, have not read a single sentence on the topic. I have never thought about my electrolytes, my metabolites, or my need for special shoes. I cannot draw upon any previous experiences because nothing I've done even remotely relates to doing a marathon. I've never run, jogged, biked, skied, skated, bladed, or done anything where my feet go fast, either on their own or with things strapped to them. In fact, that has always been my litmus test for any new activity that has come my way—if my feet go fast, the activity is not for me.

Everything is relative. A walk in the park for one person may be like climbing a mountain for another. Walking 26.2 miles might sound easy to some and inconceivable to others. I don't know how it sounds to me. Having not put any miles under my belt it probably should sound difficult. For some reason, though, it does not strike me as a monumental feat that is completely out of the question. This may change when I actually start walking but sitting here at my desk, it sounds do-able. I've marched around Disneyland for more than eight hours. I should be able to march around Portland.

I think my preparation strategy is not going to involve reading everything I can about the subject of marathons. I would get confused and discouraged, unable to separate fact from fiction. My plan is to stay ignorant and see what issues and obstacles present themselves as I begin to train. I'll customize my preparation based upon my needs, not by slick marketing ads showing hard, fit, young athletes breezing through their marathon miles with the aid of special marathon-enhancing products. Knowing me, I would be conned into thinking that I, too, am a hard, fit, young athlete, and I would waste a lot of money. I may end up being the most unorthodox marathon participant in Portland, or I may come to the conclusion that I need every specialty item known to the marathoning world. I will start with good shoes that comfortably house my orthotics and go from there.

# *Packing the Fanny Pack*

Never having participated in a marathon before, I'm unclear what you need to have in your possession on the actual race day (I'm using the term "race" loosely). I'll have to put some thought into this. I don't want to find myself in the middle of the marathon lacking some critical piece. I realize I must pack light, but I must not undertake this without having close at hand the essential, vital items I will need during this arduous day.

On race day, I would like to have strapped to my body a lightweight jacket in case it rains, a cell phone for emergencies, an iPod to pass the time, perhaps a change of socks, Chapstick, a piece of identification in case I wander off the route in an electrolyte-imbalanced stupor, and plenty of snacks. I wonder what kind of snacks I should bring? I have images of tables with drinks set up along a running route and cups all over the pavement. I'm assuming this will be the case in Portland so I don't think I need to pack beverages. But I don't have images of snack tables along a running route. Snacks are very important to me when I do any traveling, and 26.2 miles constitutes traveling. Since I'm walking, I'm not concerned about choking or being unable to handle a nice snack. If I were running, snacks would be out of the question. But walking a marathon should allow for snacking. After all, I need to keep my energy up. M&Ms sound good. Gummy bears might be nice. Maybe something salty like pretzels or nuts. I don't think there's time for a lunch stop so I'll need enough snacks to get me through the day.

I found an old fanny pack in the closet and tried it on, thinking that it could hold some nice snacks for the marathon. I have too much fanny for the fanny pack. I can't get it buckled. Perhaps snacking is something I should re-think—starting today.

As I really start putting some thought into marathon preparation, an image frequently comes to mind. It's from an Olympics I watched on TV years ago. A marathon runner comes into the stadium weaving and limping, bent to one side, barely putting one foot in front of the other. She looks like she had a stroke during the previous 25 miles. Now that I write this, I don't recall if it was a man or woman, but my memory is that of a woman. This poor skinny runner looks incoherent and confused, finally collapsing in a heap on the track. The crowd cheers. She is spent. She has nothing left. I don't even remember if she made it over the finish line. I just remember her giving everything she had, and then some, to get into the stadium. She was a world class athlete—one of the best in her country—and the marathon chewed her up and spit her out.

When I think of a marathon, I think of this scene, and I realize that I have no idea what I'm doing and no business doing it. Granted, walking a marathon with no time limit on a cool fall Portland day is not exactly equivalent to running a marathon in Olympic time in the heat of the summer. But for me it just might be. I might end up in a heap at my husband's feet at the finish line.

On second thought, I better pack plenty of snacks.

# First Day of Training: Lapped By the Elderly and Other Humiliating Lessons

I have now told everyone I know, everyone who would listen, that I'm getting in shape and completing the Portland Marathon seven months from now. I am officially committed. My pride and credibility are on the line. My good name is at stake. I have given my word. My word is my bond. I am honor bound. Generally, I'm full of shit but for some reason my friends and family are disregarding this fact and taking me at my word. What is up with that?

Now that I'm faced with walking 26.2 miles in a single day, my first reaction is a typical one for me—how hard can this be? Push comes to shove, I can do anything for a few hours. I had this same naïve approach to childbirth the first time around. I can handle anything, even excruciating pain, for a few hours. By hour six I was ready to jump out of the hospital window and hurtle myself and my unborn son onto the 405 freeway. An eight story freefall seemed like a good option at the time. So, although my shoot-from-the-hip assumption is always "this can't be <u>that</u> tough", I have learned that some things are, in fact, really hard. I'm going to assume, just for the sake of argument, for me, walking a marathon is one of those really hard things. Therefore, my marathon training will involve methodical planning and meticulous preparation.

Step 1: basic math. I need to complete 26.2 miles in eight hours. It's my understanding that the marathon committee folds up their tents after eight hours. Unless I want to wander across the finish line alone, I should try to complete the task in eight hours. A 15 minute mile for eight hours would result in 32 miles—way too many miles. A 20 minute mile would yield 24 miles in eight hours—not quite enough. So somewhere in between is what I'm shooting for. If I train at a 15 minute per mile pace, then I should be safe. Currently, with no miles under my belt, this doesn't sound so bad. I'm sure I'm missing something here because entire books have been written on marathon pacing, and I just figured it out in about five sentences. I know I'm not taking into account fatigue, potty breaks, hills, and a fluctuating pace. I'm sure these factors will come into my planning once I actually put on sneakers and start walking. But for now, I figure a 15 minute mile is what I need to be aiming for.

Step 2: start walking. There's a park near my son's preschool with a half mile loop walking path. It is on this path that I recently took my first baby steps toward better health. These were the first steps of approximately a million steps leading up to the marathon on October 1st. My plan for my first outing is six laps, three miles, in 45 minutes (see Step 1, basic math, above).

Mission accomplished (thank you, President Bush, for resurrecting this apropos saying). I reached my first day's goal: three miles in almost 45 minutes. Actually, it took me 50 minutes, but I'm going to count it as a successful maiden voyage. I learned several things that first day. First, a 15 minute mile is a good clip. I'm not sure my legs ever moved that fast before. Second, I hate spry elderly people. Two old duffers passed me like I was standing still, and they were chatting as they lapped me. I could not have spoken a sentence, I was puffing so hard. I had uncharitable thoughts about those seniors, yet someday I hope to be an annoyingly spry geezer myself. Third, jeans and a turtle neck get hot after just a few minutes. I need to think through my athletic apparel a little more carefully.

Mission not exactly accomplished. The next day I couldn't walk. My knees hurt, my ankles ached, my inner thighs were chafed from all the friction, and I was limping.

Step 2 modified: try swimming. Low impact exercise might be a good place to begin. The biggest problem I have with swimming is putting on my bathing suit and walking from the ladies locker room to the pool and back. Unless I rent the entire health club and throw out all the other members, I'm going to have to expose myself in public. This won't be pretty. My swimsuit is a size 18, and it's a tight fit. I am testing the tensile strength of polyester. The walk to the pool is a test of inner strength, but I do it. I look straight ahead, don't catch anyone's eye, march straight to the lap pool, and pray to God I don't run into someone I know.

Swimming is a success. I do 34 lengths of the 25 yard pool in about 25 minutes. A few days later I'm up to 50 lengths in 38 minutes. In a week I'm at 56 lengths in 45 minutes. I recently learned that 36 lengths is half a mile. I'm proud and feeling rather athletic. I don't know how this equates to walking a marathon, but it feels like it should.

With this, my marathon training has officially started. I'm out of the starting gate and actually moving, propelling myself along without the aid of wheels, a motor or a horse. Granted, I'm moving through water and not upright on my own two feet yet, but I'm getting there.

# Stretching and Sweating: Athlete or Pig?

Now that I'm an athlete, I'm noticing the things that athletes do. Two things in particular have caught my attention—stretching and sweating. I have heard many times over the years that stretching is a good thing. A must. You really need to wake up the muscles you intend to use and loosen them up. It's your obligation to let them know that they will soon be engaged in activity. It's your duty to give them a heads up that they are about to be called upon to perform their job and pull their weight. My understanding is that, if you surprise some of these muscle groups, they become either very cranky and sore, or they jump into action ready to oblige and then hurt themselves. So stretching is a way of being polite and courteous to these important body parts.

If anybody should be stretching, it should be us chubby new athletes. The muscles we are intending to use haven't been called upon in years. They are buried deep under a cushion of warm adipose tissue and water, snug as a bug and sound asleep. Picture cute little newborn-like striated muscles, happily curled up against firm comforting bones, tucked in up to their little noses in cozy layers of fat. Stretching allows us to gently awaken them, give them a tender nuzzle, and let them know that we would love to have them come out and play with us. These are delicate, unused, unprepared muscles that must be treated with the utmost respect and kindness.

But I never see overweight people doing some good stretching before hopping on the stationary bike, using the elliptical machine, or marching on the treadmill. They (i.e., me) want to begin and end our athletic endeavor unseen and unnoticed. Stretching would call attention to ourselves. But, it's more than that. There's a feeling that we don't deserve to stretch. We haven't earned the right to stretch. Look around. Only the fit, firm, sculpted athletes are doing all the stretching. Stretching is being done by the people with muscles we can all see—well defined muscles that are obviously called upon daily to strut their stuff. I would look ridiculous going through the same stretching rituals as my buff counterparts and feel completely unworthy to be performing the moves.

So, unfortunately, the emergent muscles on us novice athletes must not only jump to attention with no warning but must also perform work that they are completely unprepared to do. Life just isn't fair in the gym.

Public sweating is something else that is intriguing. Having never worked up a sweat before, I'm now noticing just how many people are perspiring around me. I was recently in a Subway sandwich shop, waiting in line with my three-year-old to order sandwiches. In front of us were two young men in their twenties or thirties with their gym bags over their shoulders and racket ball rackets sticking out the back. They had obviously just completed a rigorous match before lunch. And they were sweating profusely. The Subway was crowded, the line was slow, and no one gave them a second glance. These guys were dripping with sweat. Literally dripping pools of perspiration on the floor. One guy was dripping so much, it was splashing into his own personal puddle, and I had to step back so as not to get wet. The sweat wasn't slowly rolling down his leg. It was dripping off him from somewhere above the knee. His baggy shorts were soaked, and the drips were coming so fast and hard I thought for a moment he might have lost control of his bladder without realizing it. I was wondering whether this presented a health hazard when I looked down and, sure enough, my young son was walking through the puddle with an untied shoe. As I pulled him toward me and bent down to tie his shoe, my fingers were now wrapped around laces soaked in this guy's bodily fluids. I'm now wiping my hands on my jeans and looking around. No one seems to notice or care that we are all splashing in some stranger's sweat. He's an athlete modeling a healthy lifestyle, and his sweat confirms this. He is welcomed among us.

If I, an overweight middle-aged woman, had just exercised and went into Subway dripping puddles of hard-earned sweat onto the floor, I would be labeled disgusting. I would be sweating like a pig, not like an athlete. People would back away and whisper. I would probably be asked to leave.

I'm not sure what this all means except that a double standard is emerging. One that I didn't realize existed until I started exercising. A fit, beautiful person can sweat profusely in public, drip their bodily fluid all over our common space, and nobody has a problem with it. An overweight plain Jane sweats profusely in public, and she's gross. I feel I must fight this injustice. This is my plan. I will put on my shorts and tank top, exercise until I'm sweating really hard, then go into my local Subway and start stretching and sweating on the floor. If someone tries to give me any shit, I'll shake like a big hairy dog all over them.

# Personal Space: Thongs and Locker Rooms

Now that I'm an athlete (I love saying that), I have to remind myself that most people want more personal space than I'm inclined to give them. The various activities associated with exercising are the first I've encountered—that I can think of, anyway—that put me together with other people that don't consider themselves to be together. We're together, but we're not together. I'm now undressing, swimming, showering, soaking, sweating, walking, blow drying my hair and doing all sorts of personal things in close proximity with other people, yet we pretend we're alone. As humans, we weave through our daily routine, shifting between being social animals and solitary recluses. Some of us fall farther to one side of the spectrum or the other based upon our nature, but we all struggle with finding the right balance between connecting with those around us and giving each other appropriate space. Well, it's a struggle for me, anyway.

I'm like a Labrador—assuming everyone is as friendly as I am and anxious to get to know me. I am quick to wag my tail and lick a hand as a friendly gesture. Asking me to pretend that the people I'm together with are not really there goes against my nature. Imagine a yellow Lab in a crowd and not sticking his nose in someone's crotch. No way.

I'm now spending more time than I ever have dressing and undressing in front of strange women (unknown to me, not necessarily bizarre). I don't want to appear to have something to hide, so I don't opt to change in one of the few private corners with curtains. I'm out in the main locker room area, naked, with all the other women I'm not supposed to notice. As I dress and undress, I want to look around, compare and contrast, but I don't … much. My inclination is to want to look carefully at those I'm with, engage in conversation, ask questions, and make personal connections, but I've learned that this is neither the time nor the place. I'm especially intrigued by women I perceive to be my age or older and look great. Not skinny, or necessarily fit and firm, but with bodies that flow seamlessly from one region to the next. Legs that melt into hips and butt which then flow effortlessly north to the waist, gently expanding out to accommodate the torso and chest. Arms that emerge easily out of the shoulders and a neck that smoothly rises up to support the head. In other words, all the pieces fit together into a single package and nothing looks out of place, blown out of proportion, or stuck on as an afterthought. I would love to look like that, like all my parts were purchased at the same time from the same manufacturer.

I'm also drawn to women in thong underwear. I want to know how they work, where they go exactly and how they feel (the underwear, not the women). Is it the personality-type or the body-type that chooses to wear a thong? And are thong liners intrusive or functional? I'm curious! But I've learned that inquiring minds get shunned. I am making a vow to myself right here and now: when I loose a bunch of weight I'm going to get a thong and see how the other half lives.

My thong nightmare:

I'm slipping into my new thong while dressing in the ladies locker room at the health club. It's on, and I bend to pull on my pants when, snap, something breaks. The thong is gone. I look around on the floor, but there is no sign of it. I realize to my horror that it has disappeared into the dark vortex of my derriere. I fade out then fade in to find myself face down on a hospital gurney being wheeled quickly down a long hall and through several sets of double doors (see "Monty Python's The Meaning Of Life", the miracle of birth scene). The emergency room doctor comes quickly into the exam room, just out of my view. "What do we have here, nurse?" as he picks up my chart. His voice is familiar, and I realize I know him as he comes to the head of my bed. "Sheilagh, is that you?" We exchange pleasantries. We had recently met at a fund raiser for this hospital where, as it so happens, my husband works as a prominent physician. The nurse pipes in, "Apparently she had a wardrobe malfunction, and her thong is now lost in her extreme lower GI." "Hmm, an unfortunate mishap," says the handsome, serious ER doc. "What color was it?" The nurse comes to my head, "What color was it?" "Black", I say. She returns to the doctor's side, just out of view. "Black". "Hmmm. OK, I'll need a head lamp and some long palpation gloves". A minute later he moves back into view. Headlamp in place like a coal miner, he is pulling on long latex gloves that go up to his armpits, like a large animal vet preparing to do a rectal exam on a horse or cow. "Warm up that KY, nurse. And I think I'll need the spreaders." It is at this point I wake up.

I certainly don't want to socialize while naked, but I am really impressed with those that can. The few times I've run into someone I know while undressed, I get a little anxious and feel like an idiot. One time I had just pulled off my swimsuit and had not dried off fully, when a woman I had met through my child's school saw me and started chatting. I felt panicked and totally self-conscious, trying to quickly put on my clothes over wet skin, all while keeping up a friendly conversation. Finally, my bra had me completely hogtied. It would not slide around my wet ribcage. I shoved my arms through the straps even though the cups weren't lined up in front. I couldn't get it on, and I wouldn't take it off. I looked ridiculous getting tangled up in my big double D's. A calf roper couldn't have done any better.

It's not just the ladies locker room that requires me to modify my style. When taking training walks I find myself having to make decisions about human-to-human connectivity several times during each outing. I can't get lost in my thoughts while on a walk as there are too many interpersonal decisions that need to be made. My nature is fairly outgoing, and I'm inclined to want to connect with people. But I've noticed that I'm in the minority, at least with the mid-morning walking crowd. As we pass, left hand to left hand like good little drivers, I must decide to connect or not connect. I try to read their body language as they approach. Do I employ brief eye contact only, increase it to a slight smile, put on a full smile, move to a verbal "Hi", or look at something beyond them and give them nothing at all? All this must be evaluated and decided upon in a matter of seconds. If they are on the cell phone, no decision needs to be made. They're connected to someone else so I don't feel obligated to extend the invisible hand of friendship. On a typical walk, only about ten percent want a smile and "Hi". Most take my brief eye contact and respond with the unspoken message, "that's all I want so don't try to connect with me any more than we already have."

Lap swimming is a completely solitary athletic activity. In the lap pool, hemmed in by my lane buoys, "I touch no one and no one touches me. I am a rock. I am an iiiiiiisland" (Simon and Garfunkle). Any sound is muffled by the water, my goggles quickly fog, and I can barely make out the stripe on the bottom of the pool let alone anyone's face. Even in crowded lane conditions, I am alone. I get a lot of thinking done while swimming laps, but it's not the workout routine for me long-term. The Labrador in me likes the water, but I would still rather put my wet nose on someone and get to know them better.

# Do You Flock?

At almost six feet, my Mom is a tall, handsome woman with blond hair and a strong, solid look about her. She is fairly quiet and reserved, and not prone to chit chat. Although shy, her height and demeanor probably make her seem more commanding than she actually is. Several years ago, when she and Dad still lived in Southern California, she frequented a local nursery owned by a friendly older Korean couple. Since Mom enjoyed gardening, she was a good customer, and the diminutive owners, who spoke a bit of English, were always glad to see her come. One Christmas, Mom was looking at their selection of fresh cut trees. She wanted to do something different that year and have the tree sprayed with fake snow. Mom asked the smiling, attentive woman, "Do you flock?" The Korean woman didn't understand so Mom asked again, louder and slower, "Do you flock?" The woman became flustered, hurried to get her husband, and spoke quickly to him in Korean as she brought him over to join the conversation. Again, my Mom asked, still louder and slower, "DO YOU FLOCK?" After a quick discussion in Korean, the husband and wife came to a decision and the woman said, "Only Friday nights."

In their desperate attempt to quickly translate the unusual question from my Mom, they decided to plow ahead and answer in hope of keeping her business. From that day on, the friendly customer service cooled noticeably, and my Mom assumed they considered her a pervert with a green thumb. Accurate translation is everything.

I took a step aerobics class, and I know the instructor was speaking English because I understood all the words. For some of it, though, I didn't know what she was asking of me ("step ball change, grape vine" come to mind), and for the rest, I was unable to translate the words into the appropriate actions before the moment was gone. I was invariably facing front when everyone was facing back. I was up on my step when everyone else was down. I was three moves behind and reversed in direction for the entire hour. Trying to incorporate arm movements was asking too much. By the time my brain deciphered the instructions that the fitness guru barked over her hands-free microphone, I was hopelessly behind and out of step. I threw in the towel after just one class.

I have a feeling that this type of thing is the cause of most of the frustration we see around us. We just don't get it. We don't understand exactly what the other person is saying so we either respond in a way that does not at all reflect the original discussion, or we throw up our hands and stomp away. We're feeling flocked and we don't even know why.

# March Progress Report: Getting Off My Ass

My younger brother has been reading my marathon journal entries and has noticed that there has been very little said about the training and exercising that I'm doing to prepare for the marathon. There has been much written about thongs, weight, snacking and other people sweating, but very little about me actually doing anything. Therefore, I will periodically summarize my efforts, reflect on any successes or failures, and set up a plan for the near future. I hope this meets with my brother's approval as he sits in his recliner reading my emails.

March started slowly and ended with a flurry of aerobic activity. Exercising began in earnest on March 9. At first I walked, assuming that if I am going to walk the marathon I should train by walking around. Although this is the right approach, walking proved more challenging than I expected. I quickly moved to lap swimming. Between March 9th and 31st I walked twice but swam nine times. By months end I was swimming 70 lengths of the 25 yard pool in 48 minutes. I like counting the swimming in lengths instead of laps simply because the number is so much bigger. I love that I can do 70 of something athletic. In summary, I trained 11 out of 23 days. This is a personal record. I haven't moved this much in many years.

With regards to my weight, I am only two pounds lighter than I was 23 days ago. But I'll take it. With all the birthday cake and other crap I ate throughout March, it's a wonder I lost any weight at all. However, I think that things are changing. It may be my imagination, but I do feel a bit firmer all over. A little more fluid in my stride, like the gears have been lubed and some of the kinks have been worked out.

There's a change in my attitude about exercising. I almost want to go. (God, did I just say that?) In fact, my husband and I just had a rare date night, and we chose to go to the health club, exercise, and then eat dinner at their bistro which serves healthy meals. Normally, we go out to dinner and order anything on the menu because we go on a date so infrequently, and it's a real treat to eat at a restaurant that doesn't give toys with the meal. After a big dinner we usually go to a movie and have popcorn sprinkled with M&Ms with a diet Coke to wash it all down. A date of swimming a mile and eating grilled halibut and salad is new territory for us.

April should see more sunny days and chances to get outside and walk. My plan is to transition from all swimming to swimming and walking, with a goal of doing more walking than swimming by month's end. I heard that you really can't use another activity, like swimming, to train for a marathon. That was sad news for me since I now think of myself as a pretty impressive lap swimmer. Apparently you need to walk to train to walk long distances. Slow and steady is fine, but you need to use the muscles associated with walking. Your feet need to get used to bearing your weight for hours on end. Long, relatively slow walks, sandwiched between rest days, are supposed to train your body to more efficiently convert fats to usable fuel once the available carbohydrates are depleted. It's my understanding that the term "hitting the wall" during a marathon is the point where the on-board carbohydrates are used up (like the pasta dinner you ate the night before), and the body must start looking elsewhere, like fat stores, for fuel. So, the more practice your body has at doing this conversion, the softer you will smack the wall at mile 18. I have no idea if this is true, but it sounds reasonable and logical.

Based upon my extremely limited experience, it seems to be less jarring and easier to walk outside then on a treadmill inside. I will watch the weather and try to plan my April outings around Seattle's spring showers. I'll keep swimming 72 lengths, one mile, at the crawl (literally and figuratively). I think that's a good distance, and it keeps me swimming for about 50 minutes. Any longer than that I think I'd burn out and run the risk of not continuing. I think the most beautiful bodies are those of swimmers. I'll aim high and keep swimming.

My biggest challenge for April is to modify my eating habits. Now that I have an exercise routine started maybe I can focus on making better food choices. I'm going to start by making two changes. Eat a better breakfast which will include protein and fiber (I've discovered Kashi Go Lean Crunch brand cereal—it reminds me of Sugar Smacks—and meets the criteria of protein and fiber), and eat nothing between dinner and bedtime. I realize that I also need to drink more water and eat more fruits and vegetables, but I don't want to get crazy here. I'll start by dropping the Cocoa Puffs and skipping the after dinner goodies. Baby steps. Baby steps.

April will see the dreaded Easter Bunny hop into our house, round shouldered from carrying baskets for all three kids. The EB loves Sees Candy and generally loads up on all sorts of chocolate goodies (milk chocolate nuts and chews are particular favorites). That damn bunny. I wish there was some way to stop him. I just don't think I have the heart or willpower to intercept him. We'll see. I still have a couple of weeks to lay a trap.

I'm heading into April optimistic and anxious to see how things will unfold. I'm thinking about my jeans waiting patiently in my closet that are one size smaller than the jeans I'm wearing. Maybe we'll get reacquainted in April.

# *Trophy Wife*

The Portland Hilton is quickly filling up for marathon weekend. I need to reserve our rooms early. I don't care if they jack up their rates. I'll pay through the nose if I have to. It's the hotel closest to the start, and I don't want to take one more step than I absolutely have to on race day.

As I plan our weekend trip to Portland, the logistics are daunting. There are just too many of us. I need to determine things like which kids can sleep with each other, which need their space, which are walking the marathon, and which will need childcare for the day. I want my husband to be lurking in the background throughout race day, ready to come in and give me medical aid at a moment's notice. I need to figure out backup childcare for the youngest members of the clan should my husband be called into action. Some of the older kids are participating, some are not. As the matriarch, I'm the chief coordinator for family functions such as this. However, my official title is TW (Trophy Wife).

By most definitions, I am a trophy wife. After all, I'm a full twenty years younger than my professional, mature husband. Typically, though, trophy wives are anorexic, bejeweled, fashion savvy, and the cause of the demise of the first marriage. A TW is frequently displayed on the arm of her proud senior citizen husband who practically prances about with a renewed skip in his step. I'm not much of a display model, and I have yet to see Jon prance. I represent a new breed of trophy wife. I've never considered buying a piece of jewelry, I hate to shop, I have no sense of style, and the first marriage was over years before we met. And I have the opposite problem of anorexia. With anorexia, the really skinny person looks in the mirror and sees a really fat person. I, a rather chubby person, look in the mirror and see a normal weight person. All during the plumping phase (about 15 years and 50 pounds) I thought I still looked pretty cute. I attribute my affliction (anti-anorexia) to high self-esteem. I do, however, have one thing that solidifies my place among trophy wives—trophy children.

Before Jon met me, he was absolutely sure he did not want to have any more children. He already had three. The youngest had just entered her teens. The oldest two were already finished with college. He was done. That's it. Let somebody else have the babies.

21

Then Jon met me. We wanted to have a child together and started pursuing this as soon as we were married in 1991. After a year or so it was implied that our chances of conception were slim and that maybe we should adopt. So we did. A genetic connection wasn't important to us. In fact, we thought the child might be better off not being pulled from our collective gene pool. In the summer of 1993 we were at the birth of our daughter. Our little doll, Morgan, has been a wonderful gift to us from the moment she took her first breath.

As the new millennium approached I could hear the gears of my biological clock start to grind. After trying various drugs and fertility methods through most of the nineties (drugs which I assumed bullied my ovaries into giving up most of the good eggs already), I convinced Jon in 1999 to go for one last big push to conceive. I promised that the end of the century would see the end to my baby-making efforts. The fertility doctor and his trusty team of technicians harvested eggs, manipulated embryos, and flooded everything they could think of with hyped-up sperm. Just a few months before the end of the century I became pregnant. In the spring of 2000, a beautiful, healthy son was born. A friend of ours calls him High Tech. We call him Riley. That year I was 39 and Jon 59.

My gynecologist assured me that under no circumstances would I get pregnant again. It took years of effort, countless drugs and injections, a team of technicians, and an act of God to get it done the first time. No birth control was needed. Just go and enjoy. Needless to say, our youngest child was a huge surprise. We were feeling the love after September 11th, and it happened. One of the last feeble eggs I possessed was limping down the fallopian tube and bumped into one of the few swimming sperm with an intact tail. What are the odds? In the summer of 2002 another beautiful, healthy son, Jack, was born. That same friend calls him Low Tech. I thought my doctor should get all bills—birth through grad school—associated with the upbringing of Low Tech, but Jon convinced me that doctors are only human, and little surprises occur from time to time. I was 41 and Jon 61.

Add our three kids to Jon's adult children and we have six. Add to this the partners of each adult child, and we are up to nine. To top it all off, add our beautiful little grandbaby, and Jon and I buy Christmas presents for ten.

And so, the marathon effort has become a family affair. Everyone will have a roll. Three of the kids are walking the 26.2 miles with me. Others will be waiting at the finish line with open arms, chocolate brownies, and perhaps a wheelchair. Jon will be there, too, ready to put his trophy wife back on his arm and prance back to the Hilton.

# The Misunderstood
# Undergarment of the Very Thin

Oh, hell. I went ahead and did it. I bought a thong.

Thongs don't really relate to training for a marathon. However, my rationale for researching the thong at this juncture is that marathon participants are thin and thin women wear thongs. If I was not preparing for this marathon and getting into better shape, there's no way I would even be discussing thongs let alone purchasing one. So, tangentially, thongs can be considered pertinent if we stretch the scope of the discussion just a bit.

I had no idea thongs were such a hot topic. They are apparently very polarizing in some circles. Once you bring up the subject it seems almost everyone has an opinion or thong-related story. Obviously, thongs touch a nerve.

After reading about my curiosity regarding thongs in a previous journal entry, people feel free to bring up the subject without prompting. I have learned that there are many styles, although they all look alike to me. I'm told that some fit certain fanny types better than others. Some women are occasional thong wearers, others are full-time. One young friend, a twenty-something cutie, tells me she wears them frequently although she said, "I need to give it a rest once in awhile." I thought to myself, your thong needs a rest? I had no idea, but that makes sense, I guess.

My favorite thong conversation was with my 80 year old mother. After she read my journal entry, I asked her if she knew what a thong was. "Of course!" "How did you hear about thongs, Mom?" "The President." "Bush told you about thongs?" "No, not that incompetent misfit. Clinton." "Clinton told you about thongs?" "Sheilagh (insert exasperated sigh) it was in the investigation transcripts. When Monica bent over, the President snapped her thong. I had to look into it in order to fully understand the sworn testimony." That makes sense, I guess. Ever since Watergate and Tricky Dick, my mom follows all the big Washington scandals closely. I've got to give my mom a lot of credit. She hated Clinton during the last couple years of his Presidency—disgusted at his "despicable immoral behavior". But now, after all these years of Baby Bush, she realizes that there are a lot worse things than sexual depravity in the oval office.

One male friend said that thongs have really upped the anti at bars on Friday nights. Not a big bar patron, I don't have any sense of bar mating rituals. Apparently, with the popularity of very low cut jeans, tiny little t-shirts, and the thong, combined with the lower back tattoo, the visual display at bars is now quite interesting. Find a hip hangout that has a bar lined with stools (preferably backless stools), go on a Friday night, and stand back. When propped on the stool, the women's jeans are forced to go as low as they can possibly go, and the tiny "T" rides up. The top strap of the thong stays in place at the waist and acts as a not-so-subtle visual arrow. The tattoo at the small of the back also beckons the eye to follow the thong's mysterious path south. My husband bravely volunteered to verify this phenomenon with me. We went to The Cheese Cake Factory one weekend night and seated ourselves at a table in the bar facing the back of the stools. We had a yummy dinner. We also confirmed that thongs are out in full-force on Friday nights.

One young woman in her early thirties tells me the most important benefit of the thong is the elimination of panty lines. She's a frequent user. Many agree. Still others wear them because their partner likes the way they look in them. Let's pause here. It sounds to me like we have identified a couple of benefits.

Some women are decidedly anti-thong. There's the irritation factor and the perceived hootchie factor. My neighbor was telling me that she has a friend who recently lost a lot of weight and is now considering thongs as her panty of choice. "I'm going to call her to see if she's gone to the dark side," my neighbor told me.

When I have intimate apparel needs that require the input of an expert, I head straight to Nordstrom. One of my older daughters taught me a few years ago about the joy of a professionally fitted, properly-sized brassiere. A couple of high-quality, more expensive bras beat dozens of cheap, ill-fitting bras ten times over. The Nordstrom intimate apparel technicians are generally young, good-looking women (therefore intimidating). However, I soon came to realize that they are true professionals. Walking about with their measuring tape draped around their neck like a nurse with a stethoscope, they help you in a non-judgmental, confidential, and caring manner. When I decided to get my thong, I headed straight to Nordstrom.

I was casually looking at the various displays of thongs, trying to appear as if I was shopping for a friend. I'm not sure what body language says, "I'm not looking at these for me. I'm looking for a friend," but that's what I was aiming for. An intimate apparel professional approached me and asked, "Is there something I can help you find?" Before I could chicken out, I stood tall, turned to her and said in my most direct, confident voice, "I'm looking for a thong. I want the biggest damn thong you got." Heads turned. The intimate apparel department was not as intimate as I had thought. "Excuse me?" she asked. I leaned closer to her this time, speaking quietly, "Please don't make me repeat that."

I am now the proud owner of a lilac and baby blue striped thong, size XL. I know it's lilac and baby blue because when I hold it in my hands and look, that's what I see. However, when it's on, it is completely out of sight. I can't see hide nor hair of it.

Let's review the benefits of a thong as put forth by thong supporters. First, they claim no more panty lines. They're right, there are no more panty lines. Hell, there ain't nothin. On me, all of the thin strapping gets sucked into folds of flesh. If I had been a Clinton intern, he wouldn't have been able to find a strap to snap. Which brings us to the second benefit—partner's enjoyment. Jon had a pretty good laugh, so I guess that counts.

Despite the benefits, I didn't like it. I wore my thong for less than five minutes. I felt over exposed, even with outer clothing on. I felt like I was missing my security blanket. My big, industrial-size underwear gather everything up, cover all the dimples, overhangs and stretch marks, and unify the whole mess into one singular buttocks. With the thong, everything is loose and going every which way like a litter of pug puppies. Perhaps, when I lose a lot of weight (which I was supposed to do prior to getting the thong), most of the puppies will have departed, and I won't feel so insecure when wearing my thong. Until then, I think I'll just give it a rest.

# *Athlete Without a Team*

As I do my almost daily training walks or lap swims, I can see why exercising is so hard to embrace. I'm doing it for the end results, but the doing, itself, is not really doing anything at all. It's mind-numbing, monotonous, repetitive muscle contractions, and my brain has nothing else to do but think about how many reps/laps/miles are left before I can eat next. If I'm going to stay fit for the remainder of my hopefully long life, I'm going to need to get into a sport or some sort of activity that's interesting, requires some thought and distraction, and includes some measure of improvement. And, of course, involves an appropriate amount of heavy breathing and sweating. And is legal.

I have very limited sports experience. My dad was decidedly anti-PE and aggressively encouraged us to bail out of phys. ed. whenever possible. Athletics in general were looked down upon as something intelligent people didn't have the time to do. Our family didn't follow professional sports teams, and sports stars were never discussed in glowing terms or elevated to hero status. One of the few sports I remember watching as a kid on TV was roller derby. I'm not sure why I was drawn to roller derby as a kid, but I remember being mesmerized by the team whip maneuver and watching big buxom women on skates elbow each other in the face. I might need therapy to get to the bottom of that one.

As an adult, though, I picked up tennis, and I enjoy ladies doubles a great deal. It's a sport with lots of pauses in the action for discussions, socializing, water sips, and getting ready for the next point. In ladies doubles, at my level anyway, the times you actually must run are rare, and the distance is generally only a few steps. The way I play doubles with the ladies, it's not the most aerobic activity, but it's better than sitting at home eating Ding Dongs. To be honest, you can be pretty darn chubby and still play effective ladies doubles. This is probably not the sport that will keep me fit as a fiddle once I'm done with the marathon in October.

Anyone who knows me knows that my true sport of choice is the sport of kings—riding. With the right horse under me, I have been described in rather glowing terms, competing aggressively in the beautiful sport of show jumping. For me, riding is not just a sport, it's a lifestyle, an all consuming passion, and an incredibly expensive addiction. My dad once said, way back when I was a teen-ager, that it would be less expensive to have a mistress with a cocaine habit than a daughter with a horse. He was not far off. Riding is not only an expensive addiction but an alternative reality. When you're involved in it, every other aspect of your life is altered so it doesn't interfere with your riding. I quit cold turkey in 1998 and haven't been on a horse for many years, so this sport, too, will not be the one I turn to once the marathon is over. Unless, of course, I stumble into a ton of money. If I could afford to do it, I'd be back at it in a heartbeat. Once an addict, always an addict.

At this stage of the game, I think a team sport would be the best. The pressure of showing up so as not to let down the team would keep me committed. The camaraderie would fill my social needs. I just don't know what sport it would be. I have ball anxiety (fear of balls coming at me). Close contact with balls is out of the question. My husband wonders if there is a legitimate sport that doesn't involve a ball. He can't think of one. Even if I'm in great shape I can't run. Maybe I'm too old to learn a new sport. I wish I had some previous team experience.

I have only one small team sport experience. I played for the Palos Verdes High School Girls Varsity Basketball Team, 1978-1979 season. The only reason my three girlfriends and I joined is because they couldn't get enough girls to make a full team. Our school needed us, and we answered the call. We were seniors with no basketball experience. The opportunity to participate was never going to be easier. We lost every game as I recall, and, to top it off, we didn't even look cute. The uniforms were hideous black polyester. On a team of poor ball players, I was the worst. I have never been able to run and dribbling, passing, and catching were out of the question (ball anxiety). But, at 5'9", I could stand with my arms up in the air and block. So that's what I did. I stood around with my arms in the air and tried to get in people's way. Once during the season the ball ended up in my hands. I was shocked. Someone must have made a grievous error in execution. I got so excited I took the shot. No one even tried to block me—they were all running down to the other end of the court. Unchallenged, I made the basket. Unfortunately, it was the other team's basket. That was the highlight of my basketball career, and my last time on a team.

My basketball career is probably filled with funny stories, but that season is more sad than anything else. I can't think about the basketball team without thinking of my girlfriends and how, mid-season, we lost one of our teammates. December, 1978, Laura was killed in a car accident on the way to school. She died Christmas Eve, 1978. Many years have gone by, but when I reflect on it today, her death is even more tragic because my perspective has shifted. Now I think of it as the heartbreaking loss of a child, and the bottomless pain that I would feel as a mother.

As I finish this entry, I am left feeling melancholy. Death will do that. I still can't think of what sport or activity I could possibly take up at age 45 that wouldn't completely embarrass or injure me. I'm not looking forward to swimming my laps tomorrow, but I will. Perhaps I need to revisit roller derby. Short track speed skating (the team event) looks a hell of a lot like roller derby, and it's an Olympic Sport for God's sake. Maybe I need to learn to skate. Unfortunately skating involves my feet going fast, another show-stopper for me. Between my fear of balls, my inability to run, and my refusal to strap things onto my feet, I'm going to be hard to place on a team. There's got to be a sport out there that can accommodate my special needs.

# Second in Command of Two

Karen is the reason I've been propelled along this path toward the Portland Marathon. We've been business partners since September, 1996. Even though she and I are about the same age, she's also my niece, the daughter of Jon's older brother. This familial connection adds a level of loyalty to our relationship that would be hard to come by any other way. We've been small business owners and specialty contractors for over ten years, and we have come to know each other very well. We've been through births, deaths, injury, potty training, cancer, remodeling, real estate agents, sewer explosions, and several lawsuits. There was a time when we had more lawyers at the ready than any two women should ever need. I'm not sure if that's because of the industry we were involved in or Karen. It certainly was not because of me. I am so easy to get along with, it's not even funny. I'm the nice one.

Karen is the leader of our team—the alpha female. I am second in command of two. When Karen says, "Jump!" I say, "How high?" When Karen said, "Sheilagh, do you want to do the Portland Marathon with me next October? I'm going to do it as a fund raiser for the Children's Tumor Foundation. I think you should do it with me." I said, "Of course, Karen, whatever you say. Sign me up." I never thought she would really do it.

A month later I get a large package in the mail from the Children's Tumor Foundation welcoming me on their Marathon Team. There's an official Marathon Team shirt stating that I'm a Marathon Runner on The National Marathon Team. She actually signed me up! At almost 50 pounds overweight and totally out of shape, asking me to do a marathon is like asking Bush to identify Pakistan on a map, acknowledge global warming, or snap Laura's thong. I called Karen up. "Do you want to kill me? You can't expect me to do this! Can't we just write a check?"

Karen and I have a well-tuned balance of power between us. We have complimentary strengths that, when combined, add up to one mediocre business woman. Generally, we barely keep our business head above water, and we seem to always be involved in a business deal with a bunch of jerks. We know each other very well, and she knows that no matter how much I protest, if she got me on a

29

marathon team, and they actually sent me a shirt saying I was on the team, my ego would force me to do the damn marathon. I hate that she can manipulate me like that.

When something is important, Karen and I can do almost anything. We can fix any problem, deal with any incompetent supplier, correct any hopelessly botched job, and find a way to get stuff done. We have been scrambling through business together for a decade, but there have been very few situations that have floored either one of us for very long. The really tough stuff tends to be personal. One of the most difficult situations for Karen is watching her son, Patrick, deal with a genetic disorder she can't fix. The Children's Tumor Foundation is the primary organization spearheading the research to find a cure for Patrick's disorder, neurofibromatosis or NF. When Karen tells me that we've got to help fund the people working on a cure for Patrick and their fundraising program is doing marathons, I know that, come hell or high water, we're doing a marathon.

So, I'm committed. The fact that I've told everyone I know that I'm doing this marathon is going to keep me focused on sticking with the plan. But my commitment to see it through to the end was cemented when my partner turned to me and said, "Sheilagh, we're doing a marathon. I don't know how we're going to get it done, but we've got to find a way."

# April Progress Report: Sheilagh's Dreidel Diet

April was a month full of change for me. I focused on adding a handful of good habits and eliminating a couple of bad ones. All-in-all, I would say I was quite successful implementing the specific changes I had outlined for myself at the start of the month. I'm disappointed, however, that my incredibly humongous butt doesn't seem to be much smaller, and the scale didn't steadily head south.

Actually, that's not true. The scale did take a huge dive. My ritual is to weigh myself each morning before showering (so as not to add the weight of water in my hair) and after peeing, when I had jettisoned everything from jammies to urine. My daily happiness was dependent upon the high tech digital scale Jon brought home a few months ago. With a clear glass top and sleek design, it had the look of complete competence as it definitively and confidently proclaimed my weight to the half pound in large red numerals. No waffling, no needle bouncing back and forth, no hesitancy whatsoever. Up a half pound, down two, I trusted it with my life. Then, last Monday, I climbed aboard and after only a brief hesitation it boldly told me that I had dropped forty pounds. In twenty-four hours I had plummeted forty pounds. I jumped off, gave it time to rethink its position, then hopped back on. But again it stated my weight with certainty—forty pounds less then the day before. Since I had not lost a limb during the night, I knew the scale was wrong. Which then got me thinking—how many other times had it lied to me? It was like catching someone close to you in a serious breach of trust. It saw me naked every day. How much more intimate could we have been? What else had it lied about? I trusted it, and it betrayed me. This put me in a personal tail spin. Now I don't know what I weighed at the start or what I weigh now. My guess is I'm down about five pounds.

In April I met with my physical therapist, Jamie, a terrific guy who specializes in gait analysis and orthotics. I told him my marathon plans, showed him my shoes, and explained my new knee pain. He gave me two exercises to do to strengthen the muscles that support the knee and knee cap—squats and side stepping up and down the hall with a stretchy band around my ankles. I'm to do these exercises every day. I started great guns, doing them religiously each day, and my knee felt better within 48 hours. After five days of religion, I stopped doing them daily even though I need to do these every day. It would be terrible to limp 26.2 miles with a throbbing knee. Jamie also told me not to get too focused on weight loss. With the amount of exercising I'm doing I'm exchanging fat for heavier muscle. He encouraged me to go by how I feel and not by the scale. How did he know that my scale was the source of my happiness and self-esteem, and it would betray me later in the month?

The good habits I successfully added during April were eating a healthy breakfast, eliminating after dinner snacks most of the time, and engaging in frequent exercise.

First, breakfast. Eat only a healthy breakfast with protein and fiber. I deviated from my Kashi Go Lean Crunch only twice the entire month and had pancakes and low-cal syrup with my youngest son. Digressing only twice out of 30 days is great for me. I'm a donut-and-Cocoa Puffs kind of gal. I also enjoy Sugar Pops and Sugar Smacks. Now they call these cereals Pops and Smacks. They dropped the Sugar. Sugar was considered goodness when I was a kid getting hooked on these products. Now the "sugar" is gone from the name, but they still have that same great taste, not that I will ever enjoy them again, mind you.

No after dinner snacking. This was a hard one but I was successful about 80% of the time. There's room for improvement but still a significant change for the better.

I devoted a lot of energy and time into establishing an exercise habit. It's equivalent to a full-time job. At least it seems that way when you add up all the time spent thinking about exercising, preparing to exercise, driving to exercise, actually exercising, and returning from exercise. It's exhausting. However, out of 30 days, I swam seven times and walked 12 times. 19 days in one month is a new personal record. All swims were a little over a mile each—72 lengths of the 25 yard pool. I can do that in just under 50 minutes. The walks ranged from 1.5 miles up to 4.2 miles, with ten walks being three miles or more each. I walked 39.6 miles and swam seven miles in April. I know for a fact that's a personal record. I can't believe I walked that far. I don't even like to drive that far.

My goals for May will build upon what I've started. I will try to maintain the habits of eating a healthy breakfast and eliminating after dinner snacks. I need to find another breakfast food because I'm sure to get sick of Kashi Go Lean Crunch soon. I'll keep up with the exercise as the marathon training schedule starts May 7th. I will be walking three times each week, and I'll try to swim between walking days.

In addition, I'll try to add the following new goals in May—do my PT exercises every day, drink eight cups of water every day, and eliminate all fried foods. I'm not sure I buy the water thing, but everybody says to do it, so I guess I'll just take their word for it. It can't hurt, and it might take up space that would be otherwise occupied by crackers or chocolate. I need to address my caloric intake, and I think I'll start with a specific and clear directive. Do not put anything deep fried in your big fat mouth.

Frankly, with all this exercising, I can't believe the fat isn't just falling off, but I'm not exactly following the food pyramid guidelines either. My personal pyramid is turned upside down and shaped more like a dreidel. As I recall, the food pyramid (at least the old one I learned in school) has a broad fruit and veggie base, narrows for the starches, narrows further for proteins and milk products, and has a little tippy top for fats. Sheilagh's dreidel diet has a narrow, almost non-existent fruit/veggie base, widens quickly for starches, stays thick for protein, and has a sizeable fat-based top. I heard "they" (the all-knowing "they" in the Federal Government) have changed the pyramid but I doubt the new one resembles my dreidel. I'm getting concrete proof that my dreidel plan is not supportive of weight loss. Even with exercise, embracing the dreidel food plan is not going to get me where I need to go.

Finally, I need to remember that the other equally important reason I'm doing this marathon is fund raising for the Children's Tumor Foundation. In March and April, 18 friends and family members sent in contributions to the CTF in support of my marathon effort. So far I have raised over $1,900 with donations ranging from $10 to $600. Several folks contributed amounts that I know were significant chunks out of their spending money, and I'm in awe of their generosity and kindness. My goal is $3,500 so I'm over halfway there. With five months to go, I think I'll hit my target.

I love May. It's my favorite month. It will see my 45th birthday and my 15th wedding anniversary. Mothers Day will also be thrown in as will Memorial Day. We're guaranteed more sunny days and lots of blooms in the garden. A big month no matter how you slice it. At 45 I'm half way done with my life. I'm shooting for good health until I'm 90. I don't care what happens after that. After 15 years of marriage I'm at a loss to describe just how terrific Jon is. A better husband could not have been designed for me. I hope he maintains good health until he's 110, then I don't give a shit what happens to him after that either. My tune may change in 2051, but we'll cross that bridge when we come to it.

So, despite my scale's serious breach of trust, I'm looking forward to the beautiful month of May. The adventure is now fully underway.

# Weight Loss and Rocket Science

Acquaintance: "Sheilagh, I heard you're going to be at the Portland Marathon. That's great!"

Sheilagh: "Thanks. It should be fun."

A: "Do you know what you'll be doing?"

S: "Uh, yea. I'm pretty sure."

A: "Will they have you at the start?"

S: "Well, initially."

A: "Do you think they'll have you out there all day?"

S: "I'm sure I'll be out there all day. I hope to be done in eight hours, but it might take me even longer."

A: "That's great. It's really nice of you to do it."

S: "Huh? Ah, yea, I guess."

A: "They'll probably have you handing out water at an aid station or something."

S: "Huh?" (As articulate as ever.)

A: "You know, with volunteers that have never been to a marathon, they'll probably stick you at a water table."

S: "I'm not a volunteer."

A" "You're paid staff? How did you get that job?"

S: "I'm in the race. I have a bib number. I'm a participant."

A: "No way! Really? You're kidding, right?"

Concluding that I was a volunteer at the marathon probably feels like a safe assumption for people that know me in passing. And at this point, there are no obvious outward signs that I am a marathon participant. In fact, I look like the antithesis of a marathoner. But I'm early in my training, and the metamorphosis has just begun. I'm like the fattened caterpillar just beginning to spin her chrysalis. I'm hoping that in five months a five foot nine inch, sleek size 12 (oh please, oh please, oh please), 45-year-old butterfly will emerge on the streets of Portland.

Once in awhile things and people are not as they seem. The experience of being completely shocked by someone and finding that they are not at all as you had assumed is like traveling to distant exotic destinations full of surprises. Actually, I've never traveled to distant exotic destinations, but I imagine the feeling of discovery might be similar. Sometimes the most unassuming people hold the biggest surprises.

My older brother and his wife have a home out in the country in California. As a hobby they grow grapes on two hillside acres next to their house and make a variety of wines. Each fall they invite friends and family to help with the harvest. One year, an old acquaintance of my brother's from high school showed up. My brother hadn't seen him in thirty years and tried to recall what this fellow was like. He remembered him as a quiet, simple kid who didn't say much and didn't seem to do much, either. From these murky memories he made some assumptions about the unassuming man standing before him in his kitchen. The most important assumption was that he was probably capable of picking grapes. After all, cutting bunches off the vine isn't exactly rocket science.

My Brother: "God, man, it's great to see you after all this time. It must be, what, thirty years?"

Old Friend: "Yea."

MB: "I'm glad you heard about our little harvest party. We can always use extra hands getting those grapes off the hill."

OF: "Yea. No problem."

MB: "So, ahhh, what are you doing these days? Are you working?"

OF: "Yea. I'm with the shuttle."

MB: "Oh, good for you. The Shuttle ... uhh ... Express. Great! (My brother's thinking the van service that takes people to the airport. That would fit the teenager he remembered.) That must require a lot of driving."

OF: "I don't know. I guess."

MB: "You must have a good memory. You know, like remembering all the routes. You must really see a lot of the airport."

OF: "Uh, yea, I guess I do some traveling."

MB: "Do you have to do a lot of lifting?"

OF: "No. No lifting."

MB: "Great. Some of the stuff people pack can get really heavy. Sounds like a good job. Too much sitting for me, though. (Uncomfortable pause.) Uhhhh. Right.... So.... are you a driver or maintenance guy or what?"

OF: "Manager."

MB: "Manager! Good for you. You manage, what, like the drivers or the mechanics or what?"

OF: "Engineers."

MB: "Wow, engineers. Good for you! I wouldn't have thought Shuttle Express would have engineers."

OF: "I manage an engineering team for THE shuttle."

MB: "Right. The shuttle van. Excellent."

OF: "No. (Pointing skyward in a big sweeping motion.) The Space Shuttle. I manage an engineering team for the Space Shuttle. I'm with NASA."

MB: "Really? A rocket scientist? No shit!"

It's one thing to make wrong assumptions about someone you haven't seen in 30 years, but I've discovered that I have made some wrong assumptions about myself. And I see the woman every day! For example, I made an assumption regarding my weight loss. I assumed weight loss was not rocket science. I thought that if I got moving and exercised at least three or four times a week (heavy breathing for at least 60 minutes at a whack), the pounds would just melt away. I was assuming that weight loss would be fast if I changed my food intake only minimally but increased my activity level significantly. This has not exactly been the case. My fat is hanging on for dear life. It likes it here, on my hips and butt. It has a good home. Why should it move out now, after all these years? I visualize all this fat as a bunch of free loaders living in the rental house of my mid-section, not paying the rent, living like pigs, and decreasing the value of my property. They're trashing the place, and the curb appeal has gone to hell. If I had to sell I would be hard-pressed. It's time they go. A drastic reduction in calories must act as the eviction notice and exercise is the big thug that will throw them out on their asses. Apparently I need both to get the job done properly.

So, I'm learning how to adjust my game plan and modify my strategy—to regroup, make modifications, alter my assumptions, and move forward. When I discover an error, I'm going to try to avoid feeling like a big, fat, stupid failure. This just leads to the consumption of copious amounts of brownies and fried food. Instead, I'm going to tell myself that any adjustments in my assumptions are signs of growth and increased self-awareness.

Right now this all sounds like bullshit and a little too woo-woo, but I'll give it a try. Maybe becoming fit goes hand-in-hand with becoming touchy-feely and self-aware. That's not to say that fit people are more self aware, but maybe the process of going from overweight to fit requires greater introspection than is done by the average, normal weight person.

This is all very interesting, and I would sure love to contemplate it further, but I think I just need to abandon the dreidel food plan (see previous chapter for details), study a little rocket science, and keep exercising.

# An Exercise-Induced Imaginary Adventure

I have never been involved in drug trafficking. I am probably the most ignorant person on the planet when it comes to illegal drugs, recreational drugs, or the transporting of these products. However, I am excellent at smuggling Hostess Cup Cake wrappers out of my car and into the trash can undetected. Until my imaginary adventure last Thursday, the closest I came to drug smuggling was when I smuggled fried chicken into a remote parking lot in Seattle and dived under the dash when I saw my girlfriend pull into the same lot to walk her dog. I didn't want her to discover me with two biscuits and the boney remains of three large fried chicken breasts.

Getting back to drug trafficking. I think my friend Lynda and I were inadvertently part of a drug exchange or something equally dubious. In reality, I think exercising resulted in way too much oxygen to our brains, which caused our imaginations to run wild. I wonder if this phenomenon has been documented—exercise-induced imaginary adventures due to an unprecedented increase in oxygen levels.

Lynda has turned into a loyal and dependable walking partner. Once a week we walk three or four miles then reward ourselves with a nice healthy lunch or pedicure. Exercising can be quite expensive. Last Thursday we were having an incredibly delicious steak salad at a nice Southwest restaurant in a posh part of Seattle when we blundered into a situation neither of us could have anticipated. One thing led to another, and soon we were imagining ourselves as participants in the seething underworld of drug-dealing criminals.

Sitting outside at a sidewalk table on a beautiful warm spring day, we prepared to order lunch, when a woman bent down near our table. She tied a wee little dog to the sidewalk display of the neighboring shop. The tiny dog immediately leaned into his collar and started pulling the display (a small wagon) away from the woman and down the street. His strength and determination to get away were impressive, given his size. Lynda kindly offered to hold his leash while the woman stepped into the shop. Rather too quickly, the woman handed over the leash and turned on her heels to leave. Just before she disappeared into the shop Lynda asked for the dog's name. "Sparky Jones," the woman said over her shoulder. "Sparky Jones?" Lynda asked. "Yes, just remember.... Sparky Jones." And with that, she was gone.

Sparky Jones was about the homeliest little mutt I've seen in a long time. With short brown fur, googly eyes, a terrible underbite, and little bow legs, he stood only about ten inches high. Sparky Jones was not a looker. But more than that, Sparky Jones had the demeanor of an escaped convict. He would not catch our eye, refused all little goody handouts, and would not even consider drinking water from Lynda's glass that she carefully offered him. He just stood motionless and stared off at a distant spot. Lynda and I are dog people, but we could not engage him for love nor money nor little bits of steak. Sparky Jones was wound tighter than a drum. He behaved as if he thought one wrong move would result in an assassin's bullet streaking out of nowhere and dropping him dead. Sparky Jones was involved in something way over his head.

We were given Sparky Jones before we ordered. We still had Sparky Jones as I was licking the last of the dressing out of my salad bowl. Halfway through our meal I had the feeling that the woman had slipped out the back door of the shop and ditched Sparky Jones with us. By the time the check came I was convinced that Sparky Jones was now ours. Lynda, the softy that she is, immediately decided she would take him home. Even though the dog had not looked at us for the hour she held his leash, she was sure that after a few meals at her house Sparky Jones would be wagging his tail and prancing happily around the living room. She was confident that her husband John, a gourmet cook, could win the heart of Sparky Jones within 48 hours.

Just when we had given up hope of seeing the woman again, a different woman approached us. She leaned over our table and spoke rather quietly, "Sparky Jones?" It was said like a code word. "This is Sparky Jones," Lynda replied. The woman, unsmiling, took the leash from Lynda and walked away. No "thank you". Nothing. The last we saw Sparky Jones he was walking like a condemned man down Madison Avenue. He never looked back. I think if he had, Lynda would have jumped the table, tackled the woman and rescued the dog. Sparky Jones was that pitiful.

A few months ago I read an article in People Magazine about drug dealers that smuggle dope into the country in the bellies of puppies. Labeled as show puppies, these dogs are drug mules transporting drugs into the U.S. As we watched Sparky Jones walk away, that article came to mind. Lynda and I checked out the shop the original woman entered. It was a small cooking shop, but no one could spend over an hour in there browsing or getting permanently lost.

Something fishy was going on, and we had become an unwitting part of it. It had the feeling of a covert handoff. I guess it happens at airports which is why Homeland Security is always telling us not to accept luggage from a person unknown to you. Personally, I think that would go without saying—I would not want to lug some stranger's crap onto my plane. Let him lug his own. But I guess there are people out there who would, but I never thought that I would become part of such an operation.

I'm just thankful we were not caught up in an undercover FBI sting targeting upper crust housewives dining, shopping and drug trafficking in Madison Park. Surveillance cameras would surely have a clear view of us sitting out in the open, handing off Sparky Jones, belly full of crack, from one manicured well-dressed underworld scuzzball to the next.

In truth, Sparky Jones is probably a very expensive rare breed we have never heard of and cannot pronounce. He's likely so in-bred that he has lost all social and omnivorous characteristics common in most dogs. He's probably a fine example of a useless animal. However, it's much more intriguing to think of him as an innocent accomplice, forced into servitude by a gang of ruthless stiletto-heeled women.

I had no idea exercise was going to be so exciting! I'm sure this is all a figment of our imagination, but I can't help thinking that we should have rescued Sparky Jones when we had the chance. Unfortunately, he's now probably swimming with the fishes. Good luck, Sparky Jones, wherever you are.

# My Invisible Friend, Farrokh, Queen of Mile Two

All three of my kids have invisible friends. My daughter had a very quiet, private one, but my two youngest boys have loud, troublesome invisible friends. Their names are Drake and Trayler. I'm not sure where the name Trayler came from, but my three-year-old is convinced that Trayler is following him around the house, playing with his toys, and rolling around on the floor with the dog. Drake is my six-year-old's imaginary buddy. Drake is constantly getting into trouble and doing crazy things. For example, right after my kindergartner got off the afternoon bus he started chasing it down the street, yelling and waving his arms in the air. He didn't get far and came walking back home. It turns out that Drake got his coat caught in the bus door, and the driver didn't notice the invisible jacket flapping in the wind. Thankfully, Drake is fine, but his coat is long gone. Trayler and Drake get blamed for a lot of spills, loud noises, broken toys, and missing cookies. Both boys can see both invisible friends, so they have each other to back up their stories. Surprisingly, Trayler is three and Drake is six. What a coincidence.

I had an invisible friend when I was a kid. I don't remember how old I was, but I had my imaginary pal going on adventures for many years. I'm a little embarrassed to admit this, but even as an adult I have an invisible friend. He provides a little mysterious undercurrent to our marriage. His name is Sven and he's been my personal assistant since Jon and I married in 1991. Sven has remained 28 years old for the past 15 years. Lord only knows why, but he's incredibly loyal and only has eyes for me. If something is out-of-place or I'm acting odd for some reason, either Jon or I usually blame Sven.

Since I've started walking longer distances a surprising and unexpected new invisible friend has made himself known. He's really more like an angel. After I walk about a mile he floats down from above and goes into my head through my iPod earphones. The iPod is loaded with an eclectic mix of music from Chopin to Abba (yes, Abba—I admit it), Emmy Lou Harris to Paul Simon, The Fairfield Four to Fleetwood Mac. It just so happens that my personal line up of songs programmed into my iPod play list has my new invisible friend belting out encouragement at the start of mile two.

He doesn't just sit on my shoulder telling me to get moving, he gets into my stride, into my brain and into all large muscle groups. He encourages me to dig deep, pick up the pace, and walk with purpose and conviction. For me, right around mile two is the hardest part of a walk. I toy with the idea of stopping and wonder why the heck I'm doing this. Just when I start to whine, he tells me that I am a champion. All the other artists that sing to me through my iPod are standing on the sidelines urging me on like cheerleaders. My invisible friend becomes part of me and my walking effort. When I sweat, he sweats. When I get sore muscles, so does he. But conversely, when he picks up the beat, so do I. When he digs deep for that high note, I dig deep for that extra gusto in my step. He propels me well into mile three. Once I'm into the third mile, I feel less stiff and more comfortable. He gets me over that first little hump. I have always loved this singer and his band—I saw them in concert two or three times 25 or 30 years ago. But it wasn't until he started singing to me during training walks that I realized he has come back to earth just to get me through this marathon.

My angel? None other than the dearly departed Farrokh Bulsara. Farrokh was born in 1946 in Zanzibar and died in 1991. As I recall, he was among the first wave of really famous people to die of AIDS. He was crazy on stage—wild and full of energy. He had an amazing voice that was powerful and clear, and he and his band sang songs that were fun and contagious. In the late seventies and early eighties, Farrokh was Queen. I mean King. He was great to see live, and his music is some of the most widely recognized rock songs ever made. At least that's what it says on his web site.

"Oh, won't you take me home tonight. Oh, down beside that red firelight. Oh, won't you give it all you've got. Fat bottom girls you make the rockin' world go round!" He's singing just to me!

"I was just a silly lad. Never knew no good from bad. But I knew life before I left my nursery. Left alone with big fat fanny, she was such a naughty Nanny. Oh big woman, you made a bad boy out of me." Alright, this doesn't read so inspirational. In fact, it's kind of creepy, but it's still a great song.

"I've paid my dues. Time after time. I've done my sentence but committed no crime. And bad mistakes, I've made a few. I've had my share of sand kicked in my face, but I've come through. We are the champions, my friends. And we'll keep on fighting 'till the end." (Now this is inspirational!) "We are the Champions! No time for losers for we are the Champions of the world!" What could be more rousing than this?

Reading the lyrics like this does not convey the true joy of the listening experience. I'm not sure I can fully explain it, but Farrokh does it for me when I need him most. He makes me forget I have legs, he's that much fun. With Farrokh belting out ballads in my ear, I'm not pounding the pavement, I'm moving through music. Without him, I start thinking about my shortness of breath, my out-of-shape legs, my achy ankles, or my next meal. With him, I am disconnected from these mere mortal annoyances and transported to a better place.

Farrokh is my marathon angel. If you want to get it on with Farrokh, just dig through your old LPs and find any Queen album. Farrokh will be there. He called himself Freddy Mercury back then. Maybe he just brings me back to when I was 18, thin, sexy, and had thighs that didn't rub. But whatever it is, it's what I need right around mile two.

# *Watch Your Step: Parenting a Pre-teen Daughter*

My 12 year old is planning on walking the marathon with me in October. Although I would walk it if she chose not to participate, I'm thrilled that she decided to take this journey with me. As she gets older there are fewer and fewer activities that we do together. My role has changed from trusted mentor to transport professional (driver). I'm the permission-slip-signing parent coordinator and general facilitator of her activities. I know this is the way it's supposed to be—the slow, methodical cutting of the umbilical cord resulting in the gradual blossoming of a young adult completely separate from her mother. But as she goes through her teen years, there should still be a few select activities and experiences that we do together. The marathon and the preparation leading up to it will be one of those things. We haven't started our training walks together, but I'm looking forward to school being out and walking with her a couple of times each week, just the two of us. Walking along, putting our miles in, and talking without the distractions of her siblings, the phone, and the TV. As she enters her teenage years, I can feel the footing shift beneath our feet. Rather than tumbling forward on autopilot, we are starting to navigate more carefully through our relationship. It's not quite as obvious where to step. My hope is that our marathon journey will help shed light on the path before us.

Truthfully, my daughter is starting to really confuse me. I don't know whether she's coming or going. One minute she's playing in the dirt, with bare feet and matted hair. The next she's primping in front of the mirror and experimenting with make-up. I tell her she's beautiful and doesn't need any of that stuff. She paints her nails black. Black! As she preens in front of the mirror she stands next to the fishbowl that is so murky you can't see the fish. Behind her is the cat litter box that hasn't been cleaned in three days. She has stuff in every corner of her room. She's like a squirrel. She lives in complete confusion, saving old flowers, notes from friends, and little do-dads that she finds on the way home from school. Clothes are all over, socks don't match, and shirts are kept in piles instead of on hangers. Closet doors are always open with stuff cascading into the middle of the room. On cold days she wears flip flops and a skimpy shirt; on hot days she wears sweatshirts. Some days she's bouncing off the walls, silly and full of energy. Other days she's sullen and half asleep, exhausted by 5:00 p.m. Some days I get one word answers, other days she provides so much detail I want to find the off button. She's loving and bubbly one minute, the next she's rolling her eyes, embarrassed to be seen with me.

The way she keeps her room and the music she listens to … I just don't get it. If I could just get her to listen to me I'm sure I could prevent her from becoming a troubled youth and insure that she blooms into a wonderful woman like me, her Mommy. I need to penetrate into her dark pre-teen world before she wanders too far astray. If she would only listen to me and follow a few simple directives, I know she would be so much happier. But I just don't know if she's listening. I wish I had a little speaker placed high up in one corner of her room where I could continuously broadcast my loving message:

"This is your Mother. I love you, but don't be a pig. Pick up your clean clothes. Put dirty ones in the hamper. Feed the fish and give it fresh water. Clean the litter box. Throw out anything that is or will soon be rotten. Put on matching socks. Show some sense—note the weather outside before dressing. Instead of stepping over something, pick it up. You're beautiful—don't put on make-up. And I saw that—don't roll your eyes. Make good choices for a change and eat something healthy for lunch. Turn your radio to the soft rock station—you'll learn to love it. Remember, you're only 12 and have no business being interested in boys. Just say "no". Don't keep secrets from your mother. I love you."

But this doesn't sound right, either. I really need to watch my step. Parenting a pre-teen brings out some questionable qualities in me. I am perfectly capable of sounding like a lunatic. To my daughter I must sometimes appear like a control freak—aggressively imposing myself on her, assuming her choices will result in a lost, defective teenager, giving her no credit for having her own good sense, and invading her space with my narrowly defined view of lifestyle and orderliness. I need to remind myself to teach and guide her by example, not derogatory direc-tives. I need to use language that is not judgmental or belittling and to refrain from being hypercritical. I don't want her to feel she's defective if she doesn't do things my way. And I need to recognize that, without realizing it, I am quick to pick at and micro-manage her. If I want to remain engaged with my daughter through her teen years, I can see that my approach will need to be more open and encouraging, rather than domineering and divisive. She can like things I dislike. She can manage her space differently than I would. She can treasure things I would toss.

I'm going to try to keep all this in mind as my daughter and I take our marathon training walks together. My goal is to talk less and listen more. This will hopefully be the single best benefit I realize from embarking on this marathon journey—spending time with my daughter. I'm still going to rag on her about the fishbowl and litter box.

# *May Progress Report: Calories, Healthy Habits, and Becoming Neurotic*

The month of May flew by. I can't remember a month starting and ending so quickly. As soon as I turned 45 the clock started racing double time. I need to find a way to slow down my perception of the passage of time, or I will be 90 before I know it.

The focus in May was more walking with less eating. It's really that simple. The concept is so simple it's beautiful. Executing it is a challenge, but contemplating it is blessedly straightforward. I discovered that tools are the key to success. I need to stay away from vague theories and stay in the realm of quantifiable concepts. My two tools are a written daily log and an automated calorie counter. My daily log is comprised of a blank calendar with quick abbreviations that I devised to represent specific daily goals met or failed. Second is my easily accessible laptop with a web-based calorie counter updated after each meal, allowing me to track caloric intake throughout the day. With this tool I know how much I've eaten at any given point in the day so I can make a decision on how to "spend" my remaining calories.

I decided one of my strongest impulses and driving personal forces is to be a goody-two-shoes-homework-finishing-don't-leave-anything-blank-on-the-test type of person. I have five daily goals that are quick to note on the calendar and I'm driven to achieve 100% at the end of each day. The five notations are—B (eat healthy breakfast), F (no fried food), PM (eat nothing after dinner), PT (do my physical therapy exercises), and a small mark for each eight ounce glass of water I drink (I aim for eight each day).

I'm using www.fitday.com to track my calories, and I'm trying to keep below 1,500 per day. I started this May 16, and I'm completely hooked. It is a wonderful tool for me because it has pie charts, graphs, reports, summaries, and all the things that an analytical bore like me can get excited about. It tracks all important nutrients and vitamins and notes where I'm deficient in red. I hate having any red marks on my homework so I'm taking vitamins for the first time in my life. Finding out how many calories are in ten Fig Newtons, 24 Ritz Crackers, three handfuls of Cheez-Its, a big bowl of chocolate ice cream, two cups of cooked rice, and a bagel was alarming. Just my mindless eating was adding on thousands of calories a day.

Based upon my age, weight, and sex, FitDay estimates that my basal caloric needs are about 1,700 calories each day (calories needed just to breath, have a heart beat, functioning kidneys, brain, etc). My self-described lifestyle (not sedentary and not a construction worker, but a Mommy on the move) uses about 1,400 calories. Any activity on top of that like a brisk walk or swimming laps are additional calories I burn on any given day. So just to go about my usual day I burn approximately 3,100 calories. Walking at 3.5 miles per hour burns four calories per minute. Swimming freestyle laps moderately slowly burns eight calories per minute. Gardening and planting burns about five calories per minute.

Based upon this information I have come to the conclusion that exercising does not result in weight loss. I just don't burn enough off. A brisk walk for one hour only burns 240 calories—not even a peanut butter sandwich. I would have to walk hours and hours to burn enough to lose weight. The benefits of exercise are many (feeling of wellbeing, physically stronger, improved cardio-vascular health, and a more efficient metabolism), but the amount of exercise I'm able to complete on a daily basis is not going to result in weight loss. It's more important and has a more significant impact on calories burned to have an active lifestyle than to exercise for an hour four times a week. My guess is that in the great cosmic weight loss equation, exercise is only about ten percent of the answer. A lifestyle that has you moving around most of the day rather than sitting is about 30 percent of the answer. The remaining 60 percent of the equation is all about calories consumed.

I started May with some behavior goals which I think are good and worthwhile (no eating after dinner, cut out fried food, drink more water), but I was still consuming a lot of calories. Portions were limitless in size as long as it was at a meal and it wasn't fried. Once FitDay came into the picture I realized I was consuming an incredible amount of food.

So, what's the bottom line? I exercised 18 days out of 31 in May, walking 16 days and swimming two. I walked over 55 miles, up from 39 miles in April and about 54 more than last May. I'm doing longer walks and starting to get a taste of what a marathon might feel like. Many more miles are in my future but so far, so good. My feet are holding up great, my back is pain-free, and all my joints are still functioning well.

From mid-March to May 31 I've lost ten pounds which on average is about a pound a week. However, as I write this on June 5th I've lost another four pounds just in the past five days. As an aside, I can now put on my fanny pack without a problem. This was not possible ten weeks ago. Maintaining calories below 1,500 and keeping active are starting to pay dividends.

When I think of my metabolism I think of a wood burning furnace (actually, I heard this somewhere but I don't remember where). A burning furnace (my metabolism) needs fuel which is food eaten plus any stored fat. To get the fire going and have it burn hot enough to burn my fat, I need to eat. This, I believe, is why starvation diets don't work. You need food to get the fire going. Maybe food is like kindling. The fat stores that I'm trying to get rid of are like the big logs in the furnace. The only way I'm going to burn those guys is to get a hot fire going and keep it burning throughout the day. Finally, fire needs oxygen. In my analogy, exercising provides the oxygen to the fire. Exercising makes my personal furnace more efficient. With exercise I am able to burn each piece of wood down to ashes rather than leaving wood in the furnace unburned. Muscle exercises and creates the oxygen for my metabolic fire. The more muscle I have, the more oxygen I'm able to supply to my furnace. Plus, the more muscles I have working the more fuel they need to do their job. I definitely have more muscle than I used to. This, I believe, is the biggest benefit of exercise as it relates to weight loss. More of my body is active tissue, using up fuel, and keeping the metabolic furnace oxygenated. This may be completely erroneous, but it's a visual that helps me understand what might be going on. If this is not what's going on, I'm going to pretend this is what's going on.

My perception of walking has changed dramatically. Now I consider a two or three mile walk something nice that I can easily fit in between other chores or errands. I throw those "little" walks in as a relaxing bonus. A month ago I would need to gear up mentally and physically to take a two mile walk, that being my big exercise of the day. During May my neighbor Patty and I walked down to the lake, had a light lunch and walked back—seven miles round trip, up-hill one way. I would have never considered such a walk a couple of months ago.

May was another turning point for me, and I'm excited to continue what has been started. June will see kids at home full-time, sunny and warm days, and two family trips. Traveling, dining out, and kids on summer break will change the rhythm of my days and test my ability to stick to my routine. I'm on a roll now and can't wait to see how I do.

# Hydration, Toenails and Other Warnings

Since I have not yet wavered from my goal of walking the Portland Marathon on October 1st, I think my family and friends are becoming increasingly convinced that I may actually do it. Or at least attempt it. A few months ago I could just as easily have said, "I'm going to learn Mandarin by October" or "I'm joining the nunnery in October" and each of these would have seemed just as likely as "I'm going to do a marathon in October". But, barring any unforeseen incident, I think I will be walking 26.2 miles in just a few months. And so, as the date draws near, I am starting to get helpful advice and grave warnings. Since I'm a blank slate on the subject, I take all such information seriously. I evaluate the advice or warning, discuss it with Jon if I have a medical question, and then determine if it applies to me. I either take action or file it away. Here are a few pearls of wisdom I've received so far.

Advice—Wear Your Marathon Outfit For An Entire Day Before Race Day

About a week prior to the marathon, wear the exact outfit you plan to wear on race day. From breakfast to dinner wear the exact under garments, shorts, t-shirt, socks, shoes, visor, fanny pack, water bottle holder, and anything else that will be on your person for the duration of the marathon. This is to prevent any surprises—seams don't hit you wrong, shorts don't ride up, bra straps don't fall down, and nothing you wear is going to bug the heck out of you if worn for eight or more hours. Don't do this dry run too far in advance because your body may change a bit and any weather variance may alter how things feel. A week or so will give you time to make any modifications to your gear and try a dry run all over again. This comes from a couple of people who have experienced long walks or runs. I think this is sound advice, and I intend to follow it. I've put it on the calendar. September 20th—wear marathon outfit all day.

Warning—Your Toenails Will Fall Off.

No ifs, ands, or buts. Your toenails will fall off. Period. At the end of walking 26.2 miles the toenails will be so bruised and traumatized that they will turn black and fall off soon after getting home from the marathon. This warning came from the neighbor of my business partner. Since then, two others have also said this is possible. I don't know about anybody else, but this sounds awful. The tender baby skin that resides under my nails is not intended to be exposed, let alone traumatized. Doesn't it take months and months to grow a whole new toenail? This would not be a minor little problem. This would be a major pain in the ass. Since this falls under medical, I consulted my husband. Jon feels any trauma to the toenails would be the result of ill-fitting shoes that are either too tight or too loose. The toes should not have excessive pressure from being crammed into a small space. This can also happen if your shoe cannot accommodate thick socks. The foot should not move around too much in a loose shoe either allowing the toes to bang repeatedly against the front of the shoe. He disagrees that losing your toenails is an inevitable part of walking a marathon. As long as my shoes fit properly I should be in good shape. As my training walks become longer, I'm going to keep on the look out for any signs of this problem. I don't want to end up in traction with no toenails.

Advice—Put Duct Tape On Your Feet To Prevent Blisters.

As most of us know, duct tape can be used to fix almost anything. In this case, it can be used as a prophylactic approach to preventing blisters. (By the way, I like being able to use the word prophylactic.) Blisters are caused by friction and heat, the result of repetitive rubbing of your skin in the shoe. Even with the best fitting shoe and the softest sock, there is going to be some movement against the skin during a 26.2 mile walk. With duct tape in place, the friction is kept away from the skin. I have heard this from several people. I wonder, though, if there are other problems that arise from having duct tape, a non-breathable layer, against the skin for so long. I'll have to try this out before race day and see how it feels. I wonder if I should duct tape my thighs? The marathon medical team would most likely need to anaesthetize me should I end up in their care and they need to take it off. But given the amount of friction happening between my thighs, it might be worth it.

Warning—Your Nipples Will Bleed.

First, I want to go on record as saying that I refuse to participate in any activity where my nipples will end up bleeding. I don't care how many people I disappoint, I ain't doin' it! And anyone who knowingly signs up for such an activity should seriously question their motivation and sanity. Having said this, I've heard from two reliable sources that men, in particular, are at risk for having raw, bleeding nipples at the end of a marathon. Again, this goes back to friction against a surface that is not accustomed to friction. In the case of men, it would be the result of having a sweaty shirt rubbing over the nipples for hours at a time. For women, it would be the result of wearing an ill-fitting bra (or no bra) that allowed the breasts to move against material for hours on end while doing the marathon. This problem, thank God, does not apply to me. My girls are stuffed into a sports bra that smashes them down and pulls them together, forming the mono-breast, one large breast-like mound that traverses the entire chest area. I don't see how it would be physically possible to have my nipples move against the cloth of my sports bra causing friction and bleeding. Men, take a prophylactic approach and put band-aids on your nipples or, better yet, duct tape. You may need anesthesia when they rip it off, but at least your nipples won't bleed during the marathon. Now, if anyone knows of any other reason why my nipples might bleed, for God's sake tell me now.

Advice—Drink Lots of Water During The Marathon

Drink lots of fluids. Stay hydrated. Drink whenever possible. Dehydration will sneak up on you before you know it causing electrolyte imbalance, heat exhaustion or even heatstroke. When you sweat and don't replace the fluids, you reduce your blood volume, and the heart has to work harder. Your sweat rate drops and heat builds up, increasing your internal temperature. You could collapse or even drop dead. Stay ahead of your thirst. Drink, drink, drink, even if you're not thirsty. I have heard this recommendation my entire life, and I've never even been an athlete. It seems like solid, time-tested advice.

Warning—Don't Drink Too Much Water During The Marathon

Don't drink too much fluid. Drinking too much water or sports drinks can put too much water into the blood, diluting the blood's sodium content while the sodium levels in other tissue (skin, brain, muscles) stays constant. Thanks to good old osmosis, water is drawn out of the blood and into the tissue causing cells to become engorged and swollen. First your wedding ring feels tight, then your hands and feet balloon, your chest feels constricted, and your brain can even swell. This can lead to fainting, a coma and even death. People have become brain dead from intracranial swelling caused by drinking too much water during a marathon. Several marathon participants over the last seven years have died due to hyponatremia or low blood sodium from too much hydration. According to the article my sister sent me titled "Hydration Angst" from the June 2006 New York Times Sunday Magazine, marathon organizers are now trying to reduce the availability of fluids. The article explains that the slow, back-of-the-pack participants are most at risk for hyponatremia because they are sucking down water for hours and hours yet they are not sweating profusely like the fast leaders. Studies have shown that the speedsters don't drink nearly as much as the slower plodders. New hydration guidelines have recently been issued by the Association of International Marathon Medical Directors warning athletes not to overdo it—limit your fluids.

OK, I think we need to stop here and explore the hydration dilemma further. I get the sense that this is an important issue primarily because both the advice to drink a lot and the warning to not drink too much involve the possibility of death. When a potential consequence is death, you have my attention. Even bleeding nipples might take a backseat to death—maybe.

Jon is firmly behind the warning to not drink too much and feels that the mantra to drink, drink, drink through a marathon is ill-advised and unnecessary. For several years I have heard him disagree with the common nutritional advice to drink at least eight cups of water a day. He has always felt this was simply not needed. My sister's NY Times article agrees, quoting studies that suggest about four cups a day is more accurate for the average person and some of that can come from food such as fruit (but who eats fruit?). Even coffee, usually considered a diuretic (something that makes you lose water), is actually a source of hydration once your body is used to the caffeine. With regards to hydration, sports drinks should be counted the same as water since they don't have enough sodium to make any difference in keeping blood sodium levels up. Sports drinks have glucose which the body needs for energy, but when we are trying to determine how much fluid to drink, sports drinks should count as water. My take on this is that the entire issue is not about replacing electrolytes or sodium, but about replacing the right amount of water that is lost when we exercise.

What do we do? Do we just drink when we feel thirsty? Or by the time we feel thirsty are we already starting to get too dehydrated? Too much water dilutes the blood sodium levels causing water to engorge the cells of tissue and brain—really bad. Too little water reduces blood volume and can cause heat exhaustion—also really bad. Possible death either way—really, really bad. What I walk away with is that each person needs to determine their own individual sweating style. Do you sweat like a stevedore, or do you lightly perspire like a prissy aristocrat? For example, I am a stress sweater, not an exercise sweater. I'll have huge rings of sweat under my arms if faced with a personally stressful situation. I first discovered this while dressing for the prom in high school. My pretty prom dress had giant sweat rings under the armpits before I walked the 15 feet from my bedroom to the living room where my date waited. However, send me on a ten mile walk, and I will only pant like a dog and slightly glisten on the end of my nose.

The article talks about sweat rates, and how we are all different. It suggests that we check our urine—a real trick in a marathon Honey Bucket but do-able before and after the race. It should be clear and pale, not dark and cloudy. My neighbor warned me that vitamins or other medications will darken urine. The best idea I've heard is to weigh yourself before a long walk, monitor how much you drink, then weigh again right after the long walk. If you dropped weight, drink a bit more. If you gained weight, cut back on fluids. Some marathons provide digital scales to participants so they can monitor their hydration using this method.

I'm very thankful to those that are offering me advice and warnings, especially my sister for shedding light on the confusion surrounding hydration. This is important stuff and just demonstrates how vital it is to think these things through.

As I contemplate these issues, I wonder about our ancestors. Walking long distances isn't a new thing. Men, women, children, and oxen walked across the country in the olden days. People walked all over the place for thousands of years, and there weren't digital scales, Nike shoes, Thorlo socks, or duct tape. How did they manage? I cringe thinking about all the bleeding nipples our forefathers and foremothers had to endure. I just thank my lucky stars I wasn't born before orthotics, ibuprofen and the sports bra.

And so, on October 2nd, I will hopefully be in my hotel room soaking my tired feet rather than lying in a Portland hospital bed in a coma, brain dead, with blistered feet, no toenails and bleeding nipples. I guess there are risks associated with almost everything we do. Even death is a possibility. But bleeding nipples—I'm not sure anything is worth that.

# Poisoning a Previously Perpetually Polluted Person

I recently poisoned myself. I ate more junk food in a single day than I have in a month. I felt polluted, like a stagnant, foul pond with bubbly scum collecting along the sides, and a greasy film covering the surface.

Not long ago I ate like this daily. I was perpetually polluted. Without skipping a beat I would suck down fries, chicken strips and cookies, crackers and chips by the handful, and a Diet Coke as a chaser. I think I may have spent most of the last ten years feeling poisoned and polluted without being aware of it. On particularly bad days, when the amount of crap I consumed was staggering, I would have a hint of feeling toxic. The sensation would swell up like the beginning of a wave, but it would never get defined enough to crest and break over. My constant level of pollution was too high. But having just finished a month of relatively healthy living a single day of laziness and eating grease-laden processed food products caused the toxic feeling to crest, curl and break with a crash. I've never had a hangover, but I'm thinking this might be the food equivalent—queasy, lethargic, bloated, and greasy. I slogged through my day in a haze. Additives I can't pronounce deadened my neurons, and trans-fats oozed from my pores. Water followed the high sodium levels into each cell leaving me puffy from head to toe. Even my husband asked if I was OK. He thought I seemed vacant at the end of the day. Maybe Sven was to blame? But it wasn't Sven, it was sulfites. The feeling is like being slightly anesthetized. Not all the way under, but in a state of conscious sedation.

On this particular day I woke up with every intention of repeating my recent good habits, but every time I turned around I was presented with a bad choice that I simply refused to ignore. The good news, however, is that I thought about every bite. It wasn't mindless eating. I was fully conscious and present with every mouthful. Although I wanted to check out and ignore my behavior, I didn't. I forced myself to take notice as to how I was feeling with each poor decision I made. If I was going to poison myself, I didn't want to allow myself to sleep through the experience. I insisted that I was a witness to my own contamination.

A couple of times I wanted to throw in the towel and not record what I was consuming, but I entered it into the log and tallied up the damage. This act of being present kept the volume relatively low compared to what it would have been had I simply shut down and stopped counting. Surprisingly, it only totaled about 1,800 calories, but I don't think I gave my body a single nutritious morsel. 1,800 calories of grease and sugar all wrapped up in a thick coating of salt.

I don't know why I did it. It would be good to identify the triggers that sent me down the sinful path of processed fried food products. The important lesson I take away from this is the undeniable fact that my physical self prefers to be healthy. The human body, with all its complexity, intricacies, and inter-dependent systems, is awe-inspiring. Given half a chance it will start to mend, heal, and return to a more healthy state. In only thirty days I can see a significant change in how I feel by simply feeding my system even moderately healthy options.

Each and every day I am realizing an equally important fact—it is not too late. I can turn the tide even after hundreds of Quarter Pounders, thousands of Oreos, and millions of fries. This realization is critical for me to internalize and embrace. It's one thing to be told that better choices will lead to better health. But to experience it firsthand with quantifiable evidence gives me hope and reinforces the positive changes I'm making.

Having said all this, I still find myself reading the nutritional information on the Cocoa Puffs box, hoping to find some fiber or vitamins or anything that would justify a nice big bowl. The final lesson of the day—old habits die hard.

# Summer Progress Report: Injured, Shoeless, but Still Walking

So much was packed into this summer that to break it down into months is almost impossible for me to do. Birthday celebrations, mini-vacations, and three kids out of school made this summer hectic and exhausting. In my mind, mid-June to early September is one incredibly long singular unit of time with no real rhythm or schedule that can be depended upon. At times it seemed like it would never end.

I had three goals for this summer. 1) Keep the kids busy and occasionally bathe them. 2) Have a few family togetherness trips and come home with the same number of children we set out with. 3) Continue to eat healthy and train for the Portland Marathon.

Keeping the children busy and content was a full time job. There were a few times I gave in and simply bought happiness—any Lego kit you want if you promise not to argue, mope, or whine for the rest of the day. I am not above bribery if it works. I counted each time they went swimming as a bathing experience so they stayed relatively clean for most of the summer. I'm not sure the two smaller kids ever brushed their teeth, but who cares. What's done is done.

I experienced a number of minor dietary set backs during the summer months. My healthy eating habits took a back seat many, many times. We celebrated six birthdays this summer at our house. Each party had cake, ice cream, and the birthday girl or boy's favorite goodies in abundance. I can remember one day in August when I ate nothing but Doritos and Skittles. Why? Who knows? While in Victoria, Canada, I gorged on the best tasting fish and chips I can remember. At 3:00 a.m. the halibut was making a hasty escape while I had to resort to Lamaze breathing techniques to endure the cramps.

My marathon training kept up at a fairly steady pace throughout the summer thanks to my friends who would not let me quit. I rarely walked alone and, as the weeks passed, the walks grew longer and longer. Walking buddies met me at 7:00

and 8:00 a.m. on several occasions so we could walk for three or four hours before it got too hot. I even entered my first "race", the "Party In The Park" 5K walk/run at Bridle Trails State Park in late June. I had a bib number, a chip timer on my ankle, and everything. The starting gun blasted, and the small mob headed up the trail to the music from "Chariots of Fire". That is the first and only organized event I've done so far, and it was really fun to be part of it. My guess is that there were three hundred participants, and that felt like a crowd. Portland will have eight thousand.

In the space of a single summer I have evolved into a seasoned walker and a rather uppity one at that. I now consider anything up to five miles a short distance. Between five and eight miles is a good work out. Anything over eight miles is a long walk. And walking over twelve miles is an awesome effort. I estimate that I have walked approximately 200 miles and have lost 25 pounds. I'm on my fourth pair of New Balance shoes and am an expert in mole skin application and toe wrapping. I now have the official walker's badge of honor—a purple, dieing toenail. My big toe on my left foot is slowly loosing its nail. Thanks to my friend Lisa who found toe gel caps on the web (who knew?), I now have a special little bonnet I place on my toe each time I walk.

I've learned several things this summer. My feet swell a full shoe size after about eight miles. Hills are hard to walk up and even harder to walk down. Certain shorts give me unspeakable seam rubs in sensitive areas. I am a whiner with no mental toughness. I am a huge baby when it comes to pain. But the biggest surprise I've learned is that once you have attained even a modest level of fitness, walking long distances is less about being an aerobic goddess and more about mastering the mechanics of body parts in motion. Nothing can be overlooked—clothing style, construction of all seams, sock thickness, bra clasp location, panty style, fanny pack weight distribution, visor style and fit, water bottle shape, iPod location and earphone accessibility, sweat management, and shoes, shoes, shoes. After eight miles, if any of these things are out of whack, forgetaboutit. I start to whine, complain, and limp. If I lived back when men, women, and oxen walked West to open the frontier, I would have been taken out behind the wagon and shot. I'm that annoying.

A blister the size of a grain of rice at the base of my baby toe can garner my full and complete attention. If one toe is even slightly rubbing the neighboring toe wrong, all hell breaks loose down there, and the discomfort can bring me to a screeching halt. I'm like the Space Shuttle. Screw up a few tiny tiles, and the entire space program is brought to its knees.

During the last two miles of an eight mile walk in mid-August I was limping badly. My shoes were too small and my left foot was screaming. The next day my right ankle was killing me. I thought I broke it and had X-rays and a surgeon's examination. As it turned out, my limping had injured a tendon in the opposite ankle. I had to wear a walking cast for two weeks. The orthopedic surgeon gave my tendon a 50 percent chance of healing enough to do the marathon. But after two weeks I was jacked up on Aleve and back in business.

To close out the summer, eight of us walked 15 miles. We did great, if I do say so myself. I think we finished at a faster pace then when we started. I felt fit. I felt strong. I felt ready to tackle the marathon in a month. We rocked. Hell, I was Rocky when he finally was able to bound up that flight of steps in the first movie and dance around with his fists in the air, inspirational trumpet music celebrating his victory. I wasn't bounding or dancing, but the feelings were all there. Twenty-four hours later my left foot was blue and bruised. I could barely hobble around the house. Jon gave me a cane so I wouldn't re-injure my right ankle from limping. I was completely deflated. After careful scrutiny I think my shoes are now too wide and my foot slides to the outside with each step, hitting a thick rubber seam on the shoe. With two weeks to go, I'm re-thinking my high-tech shoe selection.

At some point I just have to decide upon the final outfit and shoe and just do the best I can. I don't have enough time to continue fiddling with the mechanical aspects of walking a marathon. I just need to suck it up and do it. The problem is I'm not very good at sucking it up. Inner strength and fortitude have never been my strong suits.

So, with the summer of '06 officially over, let's see where we're at. Three kids are now in school full-time with happy summer vacation memories (that's good). I'm in the best shape I've been in years (that's good). I don't have the right shoes yet for the marathon which is now two weeks away (that's bad). Is it time to panic yet?

# Personal Parts and Pieces

This summer I had all of my personal parts and pieces checked out. Since I have devoted 2006 to better health, I thought it was time to get a professional assessment of my physiological state of affairs. I feel pretty good, so I was mostly doing this to show my doctors that I can, in fact, lose weight. However, living with a pathologist keeps me mindful that there can be lots of hidden parts and pieces that may turn toward the dark side, and the owner will often have no idea that one of his organs has run amuck. My interpretation of Jon's profession is this: he is in charge of the parts department at the hospital. Like the Chevy dealer but more complicated. Anything that is taken off or falls off a body goes to Jon's department for careful scrutiny. He then tells the attending doctors what they're dealing with, advising on treatment strategy, and clarifying the complex world of disease. The parts he exams range from a few tiny cells to big bloody organs. The parts department is always busy, and there are daily reminders that bad things can crop up in the healthiest of human specimens.

First, I had my annual exam with my ob/gyn who was very impressed with my weight loss. It was a proud moment for me. It was the first time EVER I was happy to get on his scale. He has been my girly doctor since 1989, so I asked him to look back and see what my weight was at my first visit. With my recent 25 pound weight loss I felt confident that I was closing in on my 1989 weight. But I am still 40 pounds heavier than I was at 28. Man, I must have been *hotttttt* 17 years ago. Funny…. at the time I remember feeling fat. I must have been psychotic. I'd give my right arm to weigh that today. In fact, I bet I would weigh that if I lopped off my right arm. Something to think about.

I then had a full physical with my incredibly beautiful internal medicine physician, an Indian woman who is smart and stunning. She makes me feel fat, pale, and homely, but she's a good doctor, so I deal with it. All the lab tests were normal, and I received a clean bill of health but was ordered to schedule a mammogram, a colonoscopy, and a total skin exam with a dermatologist. I have endured the first two procedures before and, although I would rather be doing something else, I don't find either one terribly unpleasant. My big girls don't mind being pressed into the X-ray equipment for brief periods, and the prep for the colonoscopy is much easier than the after-effects of fish and chips in Victoria. In fact, the I.V. sedation makes the colonoscopy something to look forward to.

I then had a total skin physical with a dermatologist, and this yielded some unpleasant results. It appears that my lower lip has pre-cancerous spots and must be treated with topical chemotherapy. The doctor said that if we don't go after this now then I'm sure to have much bigger problems down the line. Going through life without a lower lip is not a good look. Since the medication will make my lip even more sun sensitive, she said I should wait until after the marathon, but I should not wait too much longer than that. Apparently the chemo is a painful experience because lips are very sensitive and full of nerves. She explained that after three weeks of applying toxic cream I won't want to go out in public any more than I have to. Yikes. That doesn't sound good. I asked her what she meant. As she put it, my lip will be raw and fleshy, and will look like it was dragged over gravel from the back of a truck.

It's my understanding that when it's over, all of the cells, good and bad, are killed off and only good cells will grow back. Hopefully they'll grow back in the shape of a lower lip. What if the chemo-ed good cells get confused or pissed off and grow back as an eyebrow or an ear or, worse yet, some internal organ? Or get turned around and grow back in a permanent frown or lopsided sneer? Or maybe only half come back and my lower lip is half the size of my upper lip? I thought these were legitimate concerns, but she seemed to think I was getting all worked up over nothing. Those cells know exactly what they are supposed to look like. Of course, it's not her lower lip we're talking about here.

Burning off my lower lip will likely impact my quality of life for awhile. I'm not sure how much my lower lip is involved in my day-to-day activities, but I suspect quite a bit. And, as I've learned over the last few months, my pain threshold is low, and my tolerance for discomfort is almost nonexistent. On top of that, how will I eat, talk, smile, kiss my kids, or yell at the dog? This will not be fun. I will start the topical chemo in early October, the week after the marathon. My goal is to have a lower lip (or eyebrow or ear or sneer) by Thanksgiving.

I'm glad I had all my parts and pieces checked out. See? They found a problem I didn't even know I had. And not hidden within the fold of some unseen internal organ, but right there, as plain as the nose on my face. My Dad used to say, "Better the devil you know than the devil you don't." I'll deal with this devil. Not bravely, but in my own cowardly, whiney way. But I'll deal with it.

So, October is shaping up to be one heck of a month—a grueling 26.2 mile marathon for which I have no shoes, a mammogram, a colonoscopy, and the mangling of my lower lip. You know your life has taken a sorry turn when your colonoscopy appointment is the most pleasant thing on your calendar.

# *On Your Mark...*

Finally. It's Marathon Weekend. Saturday, September 30, 2006, and the van is packed to the gills with everything we could possibly need and then some. Jon, four kids, and I drive the three hours to Portland, excited and nervous, apprehensive and unsure. This is new territory for all of us, and there is no way of knowing whether we are prepared or not. Actually, I know Jon and the three little kids are prepared. We packed action figures, snacks, DVDs, extra clothes, balls, juice, milk, Cheerios, and swimming gear. Our adult daughter, Mara, is always prepared. The big question that hangs unspoken in the air—is Sheilagh prepared?

Six months ago, as I struggled, bitched, and moaned about everything from stretching to thongs, this weekend seemed so far away that it was almost a fictitious event. The Portland Marathon was like a huge invading army that's so far off it's just a speck on the horizon. I knew it was there and coming my way, but there's an ocean of time between now and then. But then is now, and now is now, and now it's bearing down on me such that I can't see over it or around it. Nothing else is on my radar except the Portland Marathon. It fills the whole screen. I'm going to have to just stand up and face the weekend with head held high like a brave little soldier. As soon as I can, I'm going to turn tail and walk briskly forward, hoping it doesn't roll over me, chew me up, and spit me out.

Ours is not the only van driving south from Seattle for the Portland Marathon. Five other families are making the trip to participate with me and provide logistical and moral support. When we include Karen, her husband and two kids who live in the Portland Area, the team includes 12 marathon participants and 10 cheerleaders. I know for a fact that I could not have come close to facing this challenge without the support and friendship of these wonderful people.

My marathon team is made up of an executive director, dental assistant, chemical engineer, administrative assistant, contractor, girl scout leader, small business owner, artist, PTA board member, bookkeeper, student, mom, sister, wife, daughter, and friend. But don't let our fancy titles fool you. We are warriors, not suburban pansies. Four warriors are young women, ages 11-13, who are brave, smart, beautiful, and strong. One of our kids is the youngest entrant in the Portland Marathon this year at age 11, and she uses an inhaler at times for asthma. Talk about gutsy. Some of our warriors struggle with high blood pressure, others with obesity, anxiety, ADD, depression, old injuries, new injuries, and pre-menopause. We are cancer survivors, divorce survivors, dysfunctional family survivors, and AA survivors. Now that I list all of our problems we sound like a motley crew. But we are gritty, focused, and determined. And a few of us are also well-medicated. Our hope is that some of our life experiences will come in handy as we try to cope with the challenge of 26.2 miles.

Now that we are gathered together in Portland, let the battle begin. Our first assignment is to attend the pre-race, carbo-loading pasta dinner. This will fuel us with a boatload of carbohydrates so that we can take aim at the marathon in the morning and practically fly off the starting line.

Back in February I started asking my friends and family to give donations to the Children's Tumor Foundation in support of my marathon effort. Most have been very generous, and as of Saturday, the night before the race, I've raised about $3,000 for this charity. Karen, my business partner, has raised about the same amount. Others associated with the charity have done similar work and, together, the Portland Marathon CTF participants have raised close to $25,000 for the Children's Tumor Foundation. As a thank you, the Foundation has invited us all for a pasta dinner to carbo-load in anticipation of the big race the next day. CTF is funding the research to find a cure for neurofibromatosis, the genetic disorder afflicting Karen's son, Patrick. My connection to NF is Patrick, but my team members have never heard of NF before this and have no connection to this charity or the struggle that these kids face.

The pasta dinner changes that. Although the dinner was celebratory and upbeat, it also put a face on this disease. Many little faces, actually. After meeting some families that fight NF and hearing a few stories about the pain and surgeries kids with NF must endure, my team is now firmly behind the cause of raising awareness of NF through our marathon participation. Everyone can't wait to get into their bright yellow CTF racing singlets and T-shirts. Hearing about young children facing pain and debilitating physical challenges every day has given us purpose, to try in our own small way to help make a difference. It gave a wonderful new dimension to the marathon experience. When you run (or walk) for yourself, it's empowering. When you run for others, it's inspiring.

After carbo-loading (and since I have been carbo-loading for the past decade I feel uniquely prepared and fueled for tomorrow's battle) we head back to our hotel for an early bedtime, blessedly ignorant as to what the marathon may throw our way. The race starts at 7:00 a.m. We will meet in the lobby at 6:30 a.m. with our bib numbers on, our sneakers tied, our bowels and bladders emptied, and our carbo's locked and loaded.

# *Get Set . . .*

The 5:30 a.m. wake up call rings, and I'm up like a shot. Obviously, last night's carbo loading is working. Jon and I quietly get my things together, not wanting to wake the two little boys still sleeping. We're not sure, but we guess that there is probably nothing for them to see at the start but a sea of people, so we'll let them sleep and hope we'll have rested, happy kids waiting for me at the finish line or scraping me off the pavement at mile 19. I eat my Cheerios and send up a silent prayer that my irritable bowel syndrome takes the day off. I don't really want to even think about it—thinking about it can sometimes invite it to the party. I don't want my colon chasing me from sani-can to sani-can for 26.2 miles.

My race outfit and accessories are set out, ready to go. From top to bottom, here's what I decide upon—favorite red visor; sunglasses for later; black Champion sports bra; yellow Children's Tumor Foundation racing singlet (a thin tank top designed to wick away sweat from elite athletes, not cover the hip rolls of chubby walkers); iPod Nano on a lanyard; old ratty undies (I hope I don't get in a car accident); blue mid-thigh Speedo shorts; fanny pack with two water bottles, cell phone, spf 30 Chapstick, small bags of nuts, plain M&Ms, and Skittles, six Advil and some Band-aids; thick Thorlo socks; and, the biggest gamble of all.... brand spanking new Asics Gel running shoes.

I panicked on Wednesday and bought new high-end Asics Gel running shoes. They seem comfortable and cushiony, but I have not walked anywhere in them. The marathon will be their debut. I have heard that you never, ever wear new shoes in a marathon. My other shoes had let me down after long walks, and I had lost faith in them. I need a break, and I'm hoping to get one with these new, incredibly expensive sneakers.

Morgan, our 13 year old, and Mara, our 32 year old, have their own room. Mara will help Morgan get ready to meet me in the lobby, help Jon with the boys in the 2 mile kids run, be on call for any emergencies, cheer us on at miles 19 and 26, and repair all sports injuries this evening. She describes herself as my marathon maid of honor, handling all issues so the bride (me) won't have to worry about the little things. She makes things happen, gets things done, and does it all with a smile. It would be an understatement to say that Mara is incredibly wonderful.

Jon and I decide that we will keep in touch via cell phone and meet up at mile 19 unless I need to be rescued before then. On the course map this looks like a good spot to have Mara, the boys, and him cheer me on. My plan is for Jon to get me a nice light lunch like a turkey sandwich, a brownie, and a Coke. I'll grab it from his outstretched hands as I race by. I estimate that I'll be flying through mile 19 at about 12:30 or 1:00 p.m.

We kiss goodbye, and I'm off to the frontline to enter a war I know nothing about. I don't know who the enemy is, what the dangers are, where I'll find landmines, if I'll come out victorious, or frankly why I'm even in this war. This is probably typical of most of our young military men and women. When we signed up it seemed rather glamorous, noble, and unreal, but when it's time to ship out, we don't know what the hell we're doing or why we're doing it.

It's 6:30 a.m., and my team is in the lobby nervously finishing up cups of coffee, muffins, and juice. We all have our yellow CTF racing shirts on, and I think we look rather snappy. I gather us together and take some pictures. As we huddle, we notice that some of us have our numbers pinned on the back of our shirts, others on the front. Which is right? Looking around, we are surrounded by hundreds of experienced-looking marathon participants, all with their numbers on the front. Wanting to fit in, we quickly conform. One of my teammates whispers to me, "I feel like an imposter." I know what she means. Everywhere we turn we see thin, fit, elite marathoners. My size XL racing singlet is snug and rides up, barely making it to the top of my shorts. My bet is that the majority of the folks I'm seeing are wearing roomy, breezy size XS.

As I look at our group, all shapes and sizes in their bright yellow shirts, I realize that it is not athleticism that will rule the day. It is heart. I'm game to try to do a marathon, not because I'm daring or fearless, but because Karen, Patty, Elizabeth, Jeanette, Susan, Claire, Rena, Rianne, and I have said, "Together, we will take this challenge on." I'm going to have the strength to go farther than I've ever gone before, not because of muscle, but because of the strength I draw from my kids who are walking this with me—Morgan, Laurie and Henry. Don't get me wrong—muscles and athleticism would sure help, but at 6:45 a.m. on marathon morning what we've got in abundance is heart.

Soon, we head out into the street to find the start. As walkers, we want to be near the back. Since none of us has any experience estimating how many city blocks 9,000 people occupy, we shoot for about three blocks from the official starting line. Unfortunately, we don't know exactly where to find the start, and there are people everywhere. We decide to follow the majority of the crowd and end up penned into a thick mob somewhere back from the start. As I stand waiting for something to happen, I notice that I'm facing down the street, an orientation I'm quite sure is correct, yet everyone else is facing toward the curb, perpendicular to me. And, they are looking really serious. Not a very happy group. I ask one of my teammates why everyone's facing sideways. She points. We wound up in the bathroom block. Dozens of porta-potties line both sides of the street, and runners are lined up, hundreds of them, waiting to take one last dump. At 6:55 a.m., there is no way these people are jumping off the start at 7:00 a.m.

By now there is nowhere to go, no room to move, and no way of knowing if we will ever make it out from among the bathroom lines. Our group has already broken up, being pulled apart by the crowd into smaller groups of two and three. Morgan starts to get a little panicky. At only five feet and about 95 pounds, she is feeling overwhelmed by the throng of people. I tell her to hold tight to her girlfriend's hand, and that's the last time I see her at the start.

Dawn is breaking, the air is cool but comfortable, and the porta-potty crowd is getting a little anxious. I'm starting to think about making a serious effort to change locations when a roar is heard from far up ahead. The starting gun must have gone off, but we are too far away to hear it. The cheering is building, coming down the street, rolling our way. Then I cheer with the thousands of people in front of and behind me. A moment later, everyone starts to move. Almost as one the throng heads down the street, and the bathroom crowd breaks up. I guess most decide to take their chances that a honey bucket will be available on course when they really need it.

As we move toward the starting line we hear them—the drums. Amidst the tall downtown buildings, a drum corps consisting of about fifteen different drums is beating military marching rhythms. Snares and bass drums pound out a syncopated beat, propelling us into battle. It makes the little hairs on the back of my neck stand up and a tingling sensation go down my spine. Now I know why drums were used to send ground troops into battle and prepare the tribe for war. My response to them is instant and completely involuntary. I can't think of any other animal that would have a visceral response to drumming. Why do we? But everyone, including me, is energized by them. The drums are giving us backbone and courage to face what lies ahead. The organizers of this event really know what they're doing.

It takes me seven minutes to get to the start line. The real athletes who plan on running the marathon dodge in and out of us walkers. Surprisingly fast, thousands of participants are sorted by speed, and within only a couple of minutes I'm surrounded by people who are basically at my fitness level, give or take 50 pounds. Once all those pesky marathon runners are flushed from our midst, everyone left is smiling, chatting, and enjoying the moment. I get the feeling that we all sincerely wish each other well. I don't sense competitiveness but rather resolve and a common sense of purpose.

The drums are at their loudest, bouncing perfectly off the downtown buildings, making 15 drums sound like 100. What a rush! All doubts are pushed to the back and all questions of preparedness are moot. I am in the race and, by God, I'm going to finish it.

At this point, I've gone about 300 feet. Only 138,036 more to go.

# *Go!*

The marathon is underway, and by mile one all of the runners and joggers are far ahead of us walkers. Truthfully, it's good to get them on their way and out of sight. When we are mixed together it seems a bit uncomfortable for all of us. I've read that there are many "true marathoners" who don't like the addition of walkers to their sport. I understand that because I don't like having elite runners hanging around next to me either. But it's only a matter of minutes before natural selection sifts through the participants, and we are all grouped with our own kind.

Miles two and three are going smoothly for me but not so for the initial bathroom crowd that had to abandon the porta-potty lines at the start. Long lines have formed at the outhouses set up at these early mile posts. My guess is that this is a typical marathon defecation phenomenon and is expected. The Portland Marathon seems well-prepared in this regard.

Jeanette and I walk together for the first few miles while the rest of our group is up ahead and extending their lead a little bit with each passing mile. Jeanette and I have walked together enough times for me to know that she will soon want to break away and move at a faster clip than I'm comfortable with. By mile four I'm watching the back of her and surprised at how content I am, knowing that I'm the slowest in our group. I prefer to think of myself as the anchor, the solid clean-up man, and the foundation upon which the team is built. But in reality, I'm simply the slowest.

I fall in with a gal named Patty, an old family friend of my step-daughter, Laurie. Patty and I have never had a chance to talk before now. We chat for a couple of miles. She tells me about the time Jon helped arrange for her to have back surgery with some great surgeons when she was a student with no money and no insurance. This was almost 30 years ago, yet it's still a story she gladly shares. Around mile five Patty slows up a bit, and we part ways.

All along the route there are bands, cheerleaders from local high schools and colleges, dancers, musicians, and singers. As a lone walker I look forward to each new act to help make the time go by faster. I'm also enjoying the back-of-the-pack participants who come in all shapes and sizes. Some are in hula skirts, some men have coconuts for breasts, others are dressed as fairies with wings, and one fellow is a big American flag. One very large, struggling, yet determined man has a sign on his back that says, "Cheer For George!" Everyone who passes him gives him a pat on the back, cheers him on, and wishes him well. We are all friendly, chatting and enjoying the morning. At this point, a marathon seems like a group sport with no opposing team—at least not one that we can see yet. We're all on the same side and feeling pretty smug about our ability to so easily dominate a sport that most people would consider us completely unqualified for.

Every mile or so there are tables with volunteers handing out water and sports drinks. Still confused about dehydration versus over-hydration, I decide it's prudent to take a small cup of water each time it's offered. I get a kick out of acting like a true marathoner by crumpling my cup and tossing it aside like I've seen on TV even though I could easily walk up to the garbage can and throw it away. From the looks of things, thousands have already been by the water tables, but the volunteers continue to be encouraging and animated.

Around mile seven Jeanette comes up from behind me. She had to make a brief pit stop, but now she's back on track. We walk for a few miles together. Around mile nine there is a hairpin turn, and the participants are coming back at us going the other way. So while I'm walking through mile eight, I pass each of my teammates as they complete mile ten. Everyone is smiling, happy, and showing no signs of discomfort or fatigue. Some are walking alone, and some are in pairs. Morgan is now by herself, and I'm concerned that, unless she's with someone, her fortitude will fade as the miles start to pile up. But for now she's content talking on her cell phone to friends and family and listening to her iPod.

It is at this point that I realize how difficult it would be to try to catch up with someone. At each mile marker a volunteer calls out the time and, if you are so inclined, you can calculate your pace. I begin to realize how difficult it would be to make up just five or ten minutes even with 26.2 miles to do it in. I find myself doing a lot of mental math. I want to try to keep a 17 or 18 minute mile pace so I can finish in eight hours. After eight hours all the fanfare ends at the finish line. The actual finish line moves to a side street, and there are only a few diehard friends and family members waiting to see you come in. I really want to finish in eight hours. With each mile I confirm and re-confirm in my head my speed, and I'm happy that I'm keeping exactly a 17-18 minute mile.

At mile nine when I make the hairpin turn, I'm pleased to see many people are behind me. I'm going to guess several hundred. Even though I was just passed by a woman who looked to be about 4'6" and 90 years old, I'm happy knowing I'm not dead last.

Maybe it was the old bitty who so easily passed me, maybe it's the new shoes, but, around mile ten I start to get grumpy. My feet are starting to hurt, and my baby toes on both sides are getting a little cranky. I decide not to stop and pull off my shoes. Something tells me that taking my shoes off, even for a minute, would be counter-productive.

At mile 11 I decide that I need to use a porta-potty, and there are now no lines at the mid-race toilets. Jeanette and I say good-bye, and I sit down in a very typical, heavily-used, industrial honey bucket. Rather than hovering and dashing, my usual sani-can etiquette, I sit, relax and enjoy the break. Right now it seems like a luxurious oasis. I love this honey bucket. I'm thinking it's the nicest place I've stayed at in a long time. I wonder briefly what would happen if I decide to stay here for the rest of the day. But, something forces me back on my feet to pull up my shorts and hit the pavement once again.

Back on my own I start making and receiving phone calls. Lisa, a friend from home, calls several times to urge me on. She's great that way, making a point to be present when I need encouragement. I call my Mom who tells me to save my breath. I know she's worried about me, but she doesn't want to let on or distract me from the job at hand. I call Jon several times. And I call my brother, Sean, and his wife, Lauren, in California. Probably the best thing I did around mile 11 was to tell Sean to keep calling me throughout the day. He has a nice, calm way about him, pleasant and funny. He can also deliver cold, hard truths in a nice palatable way.

Mile 12 and I'm starting to drag. I'm alone and feeling done with this whole shtick. The fun has dissipated, and now it's work. But soon mile 13 is here and shortly after that, mile 13.1, exactly half way through. I perk up and start walking with purpose, a jaunty swing in my arms and a bounce in my step. According to my calculations, I have completed half the marathon in 4 hours. Perfect. I'm thrilled! Ok, now we're talking! Real progress.

Now all I need to do is do it all over again.

This single thought takes all the wind out of my sails. There is no way I can do what I just did all over again. I can tell I'm going to slow down, but I can't afford even an extra minute per mile. But I have to keep up this pace! No, I don't! But I want to. No, I don't. I'm doing this of my own free will. This is supposed to be fun, and I'll slow down if I damn well want to. There's no one with a gun behind me. I don't need this shit. Oh, shut up and stop whining.

These types of thoughts and circular arguments propel me through miles 14 and 15. My mind is arguing back and forth, but there is one constant. My feet. My dogs are really barking, but I think they might be starting to get numb.

Numb would be good. I start mentally kicking myself for wearing new shoes. Then Jon calls to confirm our lunch plans for the mile 19 rendezvous. I've changed my mind. No lunch.

I'm not hungry but I think I need some food, so I eat my peanuts. I'm feeling well-hydrated but empty. It's about 11:45 a.m., and I'm getting my need-a-Diet-Coke headache. I pop a couple of Advil instead. Peanuts, water, and Advil. That's lunch. I know that I'm not myself because I'm not interested in the M&Ms or Skittles—very unusual.

I'm getting phone calls from my teammates up ahead. Everyone sounds good but tired. It turns out that the big hill on the course is around mile 17. They are just letting me know that it seems hard when you're doing it, but it's not that bad. It will all be over soon. I don't find this reassuring, but I thank them anyway.

Sean has also called a couple of times, and I ask him to start helping me do the math. I'm getting tired, yet I'm fixated on the math. I want to know my pace. I need to know my pace. But, I'm starting to have difficulty performing multiplication and division in my head. Mile 17 is just ahead, I've got Sean on the phone, and this bitch of a hill is killing me. I'm huffing and puffing, my baby toes feel like they are rubbed to the bone, and I bark out the time at mile 17 to Sean. I think he's at the grocery store or something, but he has his calculator at the ready and works the numbers. "Sheilagh," he says in his calm, even voice, "there's no fucking way you're going to finish this by 3 o'clock. You've slowed down too much. If you stay at your current pace I think you can get there by 3:30." "Do it again! Run the numbers again! Are you sure?" "Sheilagh, you won't be done by 3:00 p.m. unless you speed up." "I can't speed up. I'm going as fast as I can!" "Well then, 3:30 would be a good goal." Long pause. "Right. Thanks for calling, Sean." And I hang up.

Between mile 17 and 18 is the St. Johns Bridge over the Willamette River, taking me from the west side of Portland where downtown is, to the east side. It's a beautiful bridge, the view is wonderful, the breeze is cool, and, if it wasn't for doing this marathon, it would be a great day in Portland. There are very few people walking around me now. I get the feeling that many behind me bailed out. I don't look around much any more, but it seems like I'm the only one walking across this bridge at this particular moment.

I've given up on the idea of finishing by 3:00 p.m. My need to figure out my pace has evaporated, which is probably fine since now my thoughts are becoming more and more narrow in scope. I'm mostly thinking about how much farther I have to go and the damage I'm doing to my toes. My right hip and lower back are starting to tighten up, too. If I was smart I would stop and stretch, but if I stop I don't know that I'd start again.

Up ahead is mile 19, and there are Jon, Mara and the youngest kids. My two little boys run up to greet me, grabbing my hands and just about pull me over. I want to stop and hug them, but my feet won't stop. I know that stopping the rhythmic cadence of my walking would be all that's needed to stop me completely. Jon can see I'm having difficulty, but he knows not to say much. I'll quit if I want to, and he'll be happy to take me home now, but he knows not to make the offer. As I slowly walk by he says he'll see me at the finish line. It's about 1:00 p.m. I've been going for six hours. I've got 7.2 miles to go.

Morgan made mile 19 at 12:30, a half hour ahead of me. She had been walking alone for several hours and was tired and hungry. As soon as she saw her Dad, sister and two brothers, she knew she'd had enough. Nineteen miles was plenty for her. She and I hug without me breaking cadence. I'm so proud of her. She did a great job and walked a long, long way.

I consider stopping with Morgan. It would be nice to be with my family back at the hotel with room service and a pay-per-view movie. But, just as I was thinking seriously about turning around and climbing into the minivan, someone watching from the curb said, "What's NF?" My racing singlet. NF. Neurofibromatosis. I thought about the kids who can't just stop and walk away from their surgeries, pain, and life of uncertainty. I know it's sappy, but this reminder of why I was out here kept me from quitting.

I met Jennifer back at mile eight when, out of the blue, she came up beside me, introduced herself, and asked if I thought she should bail out at mile 11. "I don't know. I guess if you want to." (I'm always a big help.) Jennifer came up from behind me around mile 20. "So, you stayed with it," I said. "Shit," was all she said. We walked along together, and every time we went up or down a curb or over any variation in footing, Jennifer would say "shit" or "fuck". It's what I was thinking, but she was saying it. She told me she's a blackjack pit boss at the Flamingo in Las Vegas, and she spent the last six months sitting in bars telling people she was in training for the Portland Marathon. It became a joke at the clubs she frequents. She never took a single training walk. Right now she's very, very unhappy.

We aren't far from the mile 23 marker when Jennifer asks a perky marathon volunteer how many miles are left. I knew it was exactly 3.4. I had stopped focusing on pace a long time ago and had become fixated with knowing exactly how much farther I had to go with each passing milestone. The young, bouncy volunteer said, "Oh, about four or five miles! You're almost there!" And she clapped her hands with encouragement. A wave of anger washed over me. I came out of my trance and practically attacked the poor girl. I pointed my finger at her and yelled with spittle flying, "No! You're wrong! It's 3.4! Don't say <u>anything</u> if you don't know for sure!" The only reason I didn't belt her was because I didn't want to take the six extra steps to get to her. I must look like a lunatic. Soon after that I gave Jennifer a few M&Ms, and we parted ways.

Miles 22, 23, and 24 are grueling and tortuous. I'm not sure I've ever endured anything so intensely difficult before. Even childbirth wasn't as hard because Jon was there holding my hand, nurses would come and go frequently, and medication was always at the ready. And with childbirth, you are resigned to your destiny. You have no choice. You <u>will</u> give birth. With the marathon, you have to keep making the choice to go on. You have to force yourself to choose to continue, to endure the punishment, when you could just as easily quit.

As I walked on, my world shrank. Left foot, right foot, left foot, right foot. At corners and street crossings, I would have walked in front of a bus had it not been for marathon volunteers stopping traffic and watching for my safety. Left foot, right foot, left foot, right foot. I was in pain. I was exhausted. I didn't care anymore. I didn't know how to keep going, and I didn't know how to stop. If my dad were still alive he would have sent in a helicopter and plucked me out of this hell-hole, no questions asked.

Sean calls again. He sounds concerned. I must not sound very good. He gently suggests that maybe I stop and sit down. He'll make sure someone comes to pick me up. "No, I can't." He tells me to be careful, and he'll check on me later.

Around mile 23 Patty (from mile four) comes up from behind me. She looks at me and says, "Sheilagh, you need to eat something. Do you have anything? Because I do." "I'm fine." "Sheilagh, I insist that you eat something. Here, I have lots of different fortified snacks. Which do you want? These lemon gummy things might be good, and they have electrolytes or something." "Patty, no thanks. I'm fine." "Sheilagh, I owe your family. I owe Jon. Remember how I told you about my back surgery? Well, I owe your family, and so I'm going to help you whether you want me to or not. You really look like you need something to eat. Now, eat these. I'm not leaving you until you do." Shit. I take the organic lemon gummy thingies with electrolytes, and I force them down. "Good," says Patty, "I'll see you at the finish." I watch her as she marches on. I'm sure she's exhausted, but to me she looks like a pillar of strength. If I were in a war zone, I would want Patty in my foxhole.

Mile 24 takes me back over the Willamette River on the Steel Bridge. As I start over the bridge I slowly come upon a woman who is really struggling. I've been behind her for quite some time, but now I'm by her side. She's weeping and moaning, limping badly. One of her knees is wrapped, and she has her sweatshirt and number in her hands. I ask if I can help, and she just cries. I take her things and have her put an arm around my shoulders. "Together, we are going to cross this fucking bridge," I quietly tell her. Her name is Cindy, and she's from Kansas. "What brings you to the Portland Marathon, Cindy?" I'm trying to divert her attention from her pain. "I don't know." "Are you doing this for a charity?" "I don't remember. Yes, I guess so." "Here, let's have some M&Ms." "OK," she says between moans. Cindy's knee is popping around or something. She is so close to finishing, but each step is killing her. When we finally get over the bridge, marathon volunteers pull out a folding chair, and Cindy heads straight for it. "Cindy, if you sit you might not get back up. We're really close. I'll help you if you want to keep going. We can do it together. It doesn't matter how long it takes us." Cindy's weeping again. "No, I need to sit." "OK," and I give her back her stuff, and we hug goodbye. Cindy helped me get out of my own head where I was drowning in self-pity. We helped each other get over the bridge.

The last mile takes me through the downtown city streets. Of a race full of very long miles, this one feels like the longest mile of all. A volunteer has me stop at an intersection and wait for the light. I've been on the course for so long the streets have been re-opened to traffic. I look up, and there are Laurie, Jeanette, and Susan. They finished the race and came back a mile to meet up with me and bring me home. Morgan is there, too. I start to cry. I can't image taking one extra step, yet they came back to walk me in. After a couple of blocks I see Jon, Mara and the boys. I'm crying again. I can barely walk, my feet hurt so much. I'm exhausted and completely confused about which way to go. My family and friends lead me home. The last turn, down the shoot, and there's Karen. She can barely stand, but she's there waiting for me. We hug and start to cry.

I'm just about there—only a few more yards to go. My two little boys, one on each side, pull me over the finish line. It's 4:00 p.m.

Someone official puts a medal around my neck. I start to cry. Again.

# *That's A Wrap!*

My Portland Marathon project is officially over. Now what? How do I stop? I'll start by tying up a few loose ends.

First, my friends and family donated over $3,200 to the Children's Tumor Foundation. On one hand, it's a lot of money. On the other, it's a drop in the bucket. But, a drops a drop, and it all adds up. CTF is a terrific charity devoted to helping kids and their families overcome an often devastating disorder. I must put any complaining I do in perspective. I'm still going to complain (see below), but I recognize that my whiney little problems are just that—whiney little problems.

With regards to the marathon, I was the 7,666th person to cross the finish line of the Portland Marathon on October 1, 2006. 7,709 people finished. 43 people finished after I did. I believe about 8,800 people started the race or at least signed up. If that were the case, about 1,091 people didn't finish or didn't show up. I consider myself ahead of all of them, too. I'm convinced that I would have been on the DNF (did not finish) list if any other challenge or obstacle had presented itself. For example, if it had rained or been the least bit warm I would have likely thrown in the towel. Thank goodness the temperature was in the low sixties and the skies were blue.

A friend asked me later that evening, as I iced my hip and bandaged my toes, what my time was. I had no idea. It did not even occur to me as I crossed the finish line to look for a clock. However, the web site provides details on each participant. I crossed the finish line at 9:02:06, nine hours and two minutes after I started. It took me six hours to walk the first 19 miles and three hours to walk the last 7.2 miles. The final finisher crossed the line at 10:41:22. Obviously, I kicked their butt.

I really, really wanted to finish in eight hours. And, actually, I think I did. Just hear me out. I consider my real time to be 7:59:06 because 1) I spent about an hour in that honey bucket at mile 11 and 2) I stood on the corner three minutes waiting for the traffic light at mile 25. That puts me in at just under eight hours, which was my goal. Fantastic—another goal accomplished.

I want to note something before I forget. Almost all experienced long distance runners/walkers that I asked said that if I can go 15 miles and not kill myself doing it, I can easily go 26.2 miles on race day. This is not true. I think this is a pre-meditated, organized plot by well-intentioned people to spread misinformation to unsuspecting first-timers in order to lull us into a false sense of security. And it worked. It got me out there in my shorts at 6:30 a.m. to walk a marathon. But it's a myth along the lines of the Easter Bunny. The fact is that 15 miles is nothing like 20 miles, and 20 miles is nothing like 26.2 miles.

Everyone on my team did such a great job. Here are their times. Our daughter, Laurie, finished in 7:11:34. Her partner, Henry, was our fastest, finishing in 6:41:37. Morgan, my 13 year old daughter, walked 19 miles in about 5:30:00. Jeanette finished in 7:54:54. Susan finished in 7:24:09, and her 12 year old daughter, Claire, finished in 7:24:11. Patty finished in 7:11:33, and her 13 year old daughter, Elizabeth, finished in 6:52:21. Rena finished in 7:00:33, and her 11 year old daughter, Rianne, finished in 7:00:29. Karen finished in 7:42:55. All first time marathoners, and all did a wonderful job.

Everyone has a story that led them to the marathon. Mine, of course, is the most interesting, but Karen's is the most amazing. In January of 2005 (remember, the marathon was October of 2006) Karen could not walk across her living room without pain. She had finished a long recovery from cancer surgery and was extremely overweight. She weighed in at something like 380 pounds. Her doctors said she had fibromyalgia and should start taking pain medications. Karen decided that enough was enough. Without using fad diets, unproven supplements, crazy nutritional schemes or surgery, Karen lost about 200 pounds. She stopped eating all the crap, stopped dining at restaurants, and cut out soda. She only eats organic, natural food and drinks lots of water. She gets off her ass and exercises everyday. Karen is now pain-free and as strong as an ox. She just finished painting the outside of her house. How many of us have done that recently? And, in October of 2006, she finished the Portland Marathon—all 26.2 miles—in 7 hours and 42 minutes. What an incredible 22 months. Although not as interesting as me, she's more amazing.

Here's a brief note on a couple of other people I met along the way. Jennifer from Las Vegas finished the marathon. I'm glad she stuck it out—good for her! Cindy from Kansas finished, too. Only grim determination and sheer guts would have brought Cindy that last mile. Although I don't know her at all, she's obviously pretty cool.

Alright, enough about all these other people. Let's get back to me. Injuries? Where do I start? I was in such bad shape at the finish line Jon was going to ask the hotel if they had a wheelchair. He and Mara practically carried me back. I was completely exhausted, mentally and physically.

Each baby toe had a blister that completely encased the entire toe, even under their teeny, tiny little nails. The nails were still attached but floating on blisters. My left heal had a blister under the thick callous on the inside edge. It took a full two weeks before these were healed well enough for me to wear shoes. Two days after the marathon I developed the most painful sinus infection of my life. It felt like my eyeballs were going to pop out of my head, the pressure was so great. I started a ten day course of antibiotics. Four days after the marathon a huge cyst formed on the side of my nose. I never get that kind of thing. Coincidence? I think not. Five days after the marathon my lower back went into a muscle spasm that lasted eight days. I could only sleep in the recliner and needed codeine for the pain.

It was like my body gave up defending itself. My immune system staged a walk-out. I had spent all my personal resources doing the marathon, and I was left biologically broke.

On top of all this, I started my topical chemo treatment for my pre-cancerous lower lip five days after the marathon. A week later my lip was a huge, pussy, fleshy mess that was so painful, nothing could touch it. I couldn't brush my teeth. Food had to be cut into tiny bits. I drank through a straw. This misery lasted over two weeks.

Halfway through this, two weeks PM (post marathon), I had to prep for my colonoscopy. However, this provided the only bright spot in an otherwise dreary time. I was blessedly anesthetized for two hours during the procedure. My lip, my back, my feet, my butt were all forgotten in the haze of sedation. For this reason, colonoscopies will always hold a special place in my heart and make my top ten list of favorite semi-invasive procedures. Of course, throughout these terrible weeks I never complained. Not once.

As I look back, it's very apparent that I have been on a journey of sorts. I have covered a lot of territory, groping my way toward a goal I knew nothing about. I think I did more things right than wrong. Telling everyone I knew that I was doing a marathon was the right thing to do. Bringing M&Ms on the marathon to share as a gesture of solidarity with other struggling walkers was the right thing to do, too. Wearing new shoes on race day was the wrong thing to do.

In February I was 50 pounds over weight and hauling around the equivalent of a typical 6 year old with every step. Actually, I was more like 60 pounds over weight. Eight months later, 30 pounds lighter, and I'm now carrying around the equivalent of a toddler. This is a great start and losing another 30 pounds would be ideal.

I had set several goals for myself in February. Let's see how I did.

1.  Goal: Tuck in a shirt, put on a belt, and feel comfortable enough with the look that I go grocery shopping. Well, I really put this one to the test. I bought myself a new pair of pants and a belt (I have not owned a belt in over a decade). I went to a ladies-night-out dinner party where all the ladies were thin and fit. I wore my "Portland Marathon Finisher" shirt tucked into my new pants with the belt and accessorized the outfit with my Marathon Medal around my neck. I even had my thong on underneath. Even though I was still the largest woman there, I felt pretty good although I think the other women might have been jealous of my large gold medal. Conclusion: goal attained.

2.  Goal: From the floor, just stand up. This is getting better. I think I need to work on core strength so I don't feel my back is so vulnerable. Maybe I need yoga or Pilates. Conclusion: still needs work but on the right track.

3.  Goal: While continuing to look fetching, slip into a pair of non-queen size panty hose while sitting daintily on the edge of the bed. OK. I tried. Who thought of this lame goal, anyway? I am nowhere near being able to do this the way I envision it in my head. Conclusion: screw this. I am officially eliminating this as a goal.

4.  Goal: Slowly jog with a ponytail swinging back and forth in a cute and perky fashion. Today my son and I jogged most of the way home from his piano lesson. OK, his teacher lives across the street. But not directly across—sort of kitty corner. I measured it in my car. It's .1 miles from her door to mine. My hair has grown out, and it's long enough for a pony tail to bob in a cute and perky fashion. Conclusion: goal attained.

5.  Goal: Play ladies doubles tennis. I've been too busy recuperating from the marathon to schedule any tennis. I first have to find my racket. I haven't seen it in two or three years. And I'm not sure about the tennis outfit. I don't think I'm quite slender enough for that. Conclusion: still needs work.

6.  Goal: Wear cute low cut girlie panties. I bought some cute little num-bers and, even though I still prefer to be all gathered up in my big indus-

trial size underpants, I will slip into one of these little panties now and again. Conclusion: goal attained.

Where do I go from here? At this point, half marathons sound like the thing to do. Jon and I are registered to do the New Las Vegas Half Marathon on December 10, 2006. We are spending a long weekend together at the Mandalay Bay Hotel and Casino. I love Las Vegas. A little gambling, sleeping in, no kids, a spa treatment, late night dining, maybe a show. The marathon and half marathon start at 6:00 a.m. on Sunday, December 10th. Yikes. That's early for us Vegas girls. But 13.1 miles sounds challenging yet civilized.

I really loved the excitement of the start at the Portland Marathon and the whole atmosphere of the event. I'm planning to do a half marathon every three or four months to keep in shape and collect more medals. To be frank, I'm really only in it for the medal now. If an event isn't giving medals, I'm not participating.

Immediately after I finished the Portland Marathon I said I would never, ever do this again. Ever. Now I'm not sure. Maybe once a year we should all go through a humbling, grueling, painful, physically exhausting experience. With drums. I've decided that I want drums at all my major life events from now on. What I need to do is reduce the recuperation period that follows the marathon. Basically, I was out of commission for a month following the marathon. I'm not sure my husband would be quite so supportive and sweet if I knowingly participated in an activity that resulted in me being medicated and laid up for a month.

So the verdict is still out on whether I will do another marathon. But even if I don't, I still can say that I did it. I did a marathon. I have the medal to prove it.

# My Marathon Nightmare

I come around the last corner of the marathon, exhausted and in pain. Blood is seeping from my sneakers. My knees are popping in and out of their sockets. I'm bent over and twisted to the left, barely able to walk a straight line. I look up and see an archway of balloons over the street obviously signaling the finish line. Each step is excruciating but I manage to reach the balloons only to notice that it's just decoration and the finish line is actually around the next corner. It takes all my inner strength and fortitude to rebound from this disappointment and continue to put one foot in front of the other. Around the next corner I see an arrow pointing. I must go around yet another corner. Then another. Each new corner is a cruel joke. The only thing keeping me going is the thought of my wonderful family waiting with open arms at the finish. I'm barely staying upright, but I finally make it to the finish line. A marathon volunteer approaches and says quietly in my ear, "I'm sorry but your medal has been confiscated by some man in a rumpled suit." Weeping, I look around. No one is there save one lone drummer with only one stick. He stops his lonesome beat and hands me a note. It's from Jon. "The kids and I have been.... detained. We're safe, but please just do as they say. It's our only hope of being reunited." I'm confused and feel like I have no reason to go on, yet I must. I need to urinate. I limp to the closest porta potty, a large handicap accessible unit, and collapse on the seat, shorts and thong around my ankles. After a minute the door bursts open and in tumbles President Bush, Vice President Cheney, Donald Rumsfeld and Condi Rice. Bush, Cheney and Rumsfeld look scruffy and disheveled, as if they've slept in their suits for a week. Condi, however, looks fabulous in a pressed power suit and beautiful heels. She steps forward, hand extended to shake mine. "We need you, Sheilagh, to run for President on the Republican ticket in 2008." I look into President Bush's eyes. He looks confused. I turn toward Cheney. He's pissed and looks like he wants to shoot me in the face. If he had a gun I believe he'd do it, too. Rumsfeld quips, "We've got your husband and kids. They're in a secure location being.... questioned. You might as well cooperate. And by the way, I like your thong." Condi looks cool and confident, giving my thong a discreet glance. "Sheilagh, you will make a terrific Republican, embracing family values while spreading democracy around the world. We <u>are</u> the moral majority. Your future, I dare say your destiny, lies within the conservative ranks of the Republican party." "But I can't! I, I, I, I'm a Democrat!" I stammer, "I couldn't possibly run as a Republican! I'm pro-choice! For stem cell research! I voted for Carter! I loved Clinton!" I start to panic and hyperventilate. If I wasn't in such pain I would have jumped to my feet. It's then that I see it. My marathon medal is around Bush's neck. Condi sees that I've spotted it. "Yes, Sheilagh. We didn't want to have to resort to this, but we will hold your marathon medal until after you state publicly your support of the Republican party." I crumple to the floor at their feet, completely defeated.

It is at this point I wake up.

978-0-595-45436-5
0-595-45436-4

Printed in the United States
94619LV00004B/33/A